A STUDY OF

For His Glory

LIVING AS GOD'S MASTERPIECE

MARIAN JORDAN ELLIS

Abingdon Women ✳ Nashville

FOR HIS GLORY
Living as God's Masterpiece
Copyright © 2020 Abingdon Press
All rights reserved.

ISBN 978-1-5018-8868-7

20 21 22 23 24 25 26 27 28 29 — 10 9 8 7 6 5 4 3 2 1
MANUFACTURED IN THE UNITED STATES OF AMERICA

ABOUT THE AUTHOR

Marian Jordan Ellis is a Bible teacher at heart who is passionate about Jesus and helping women of all ages and stages of life to experience the victorious Christian life. Having a Master's Degree in Biblical Studies from Southwestern Baptist Theological Seminary, she served on the teaching team at Second Baptist Church of Houston for fifteen years and now hosts a monthly gathering for hundreds of women at Mission City Church in San Antonio, where she serves as the Director of Women's Ministry. Marian is the founder of This Redeemed Life, a global movement of women transformed by the grace and truth of Jesus Christ. She speaks domestically and internationally at women's conferences and events and has led teaching tours to Israel. Through her evangelistic event, Girls Night Out, she partnered with CRU (Campus Crusade for Christ) and spoke at 170 universities across America where over 11,000 women placed faith in Christ. Marian has been featured on many programs, radio shows, and podcasts including The 700 Club, The Harvest Show, Moody Radio, and FamilyLife Today. Thousands watch her Bible teachings and read her blog each week on the This Redeemed Life app, website (thisredeemedlife.org), and YouTube channel. She is the author of *Stand: Rising Up Against Darkness, Temptation, and Persecution* and numerous other titles. Marian and her husband, Justin, have three children (Andrew, Brenden, and Sydney) and one very spoiled dog, London.

Follow Marian:
 @marianjordan
 @marianjordanellis
thisredeemedlife.org

ACKNOWLEDGMENTS

Writing a study of Ephesians was an absolute labor of love, but I did not complete a work of this magnitude on my own. I owe a huge debt of gratitude to my family and friends who supported this project, prayed me through the writing process, and kept my family fed while I was in the writing cave.

Big thanks to my literary agent, Whitney Gossett, for championing this study and believing in God's call on my life. Hats off to the best editor in the world, Sally Sharpe. You are a dream come true, my friend! And to the entire team at Abingdon Women, you're a joy to serve Jesus alongside.

To the amazing women at *Mission City Church* and *Tue.Gather*, I love worshiping Jesus with you each month. Thank you for all the prayers you put into this project.

To my dear friends Cheryl and Kristen, thank you for creating a beautiful environment for me to teach God's Word. Becky Surber, you were my constant encourager. Lauren Walls, thank you for all you did to make the taping run so smoothly. And to all my friends who took time off to attend the videotaping, you are stunning and selfless humans, and I'm beyond grateful for your participation.

To the board of directors of *This Redeemed Life*, your prayers and guidance cover this ministry, and I'm indebted to your faithfulness.

I owe a big thanks to my mom and dad for their steadfast prayers and to Ralph and Patty for making our lives run so smoothly here in San Antonio.

To Andrew and Brenden, the love, joy, peace, patience, and goodness that flow from you is a gift from the Lord. It's a joy to be your bonus-mom. To my sweet Sydney, you were my constant inspiration while writing each day. I pray you will grow into a young woman who loves Jesus and lives for the glory of His great name. You are a masterpiece!

For years I prayed for a husband who would be a ministry partner, and in the process of producing this Bible study, I've seen how God perfectly answered that prayer. Justin Ellis, you are a gift from God. You are a true artist, and your talent made this study a masterpiece *for His glory*.

With love,

Marian

Contents

INTRODUCTION

Have you ever been captivated by a beautiful masterpiece, something that fills you with wonder and leaves you in awe of its creator? We've all likely had that experience at one time or another. But have you ever considered that *you* are a masterpiece? It's true!

Ephesians unashamedly declares that the church is God's masterpiece—and because we are the church, that includes you and me. In Christ Jesus, we are transformed from death to life, from broken to beautiful, from rejected to chosen, from alienated to family, from defeated to victorious, from lost to redeemed. In Him we become God's masterpiece—all for the glory of His name!

This one word, *masterpiece*, encompasses the breathtaking beauty of this epistle, or letter, of the apostle Paul and the purpose for which it was penned. Paul longed to convey to the church in Ephesus the mystery and majesty of God's glorious purpose for their lives—and the lives of all believers through the ages. It is a plan that began before the foundation of the world and involves each person of the Trinity: Father, Son, and Holy Spirit. God's magnificent design was and is to redeem a people for Himself who reflect His glory to the world—who are His masterpiece.

If the Bible contains a "how-to" manual for living the Christian life, I suggest it is Ephesians. In this succinct yet powerful epistle we find the key doctrines of the Christian faith. *For His Glory: Living as God's Masterpiece* is a six-week study of Ephesians that helps us understand the glory of God revealed in the gospel, equips us with a clear understanding of our identity in Christ as believers, and empowers each of us to live a life worthy of our Redeemer—to live as God's masterpiece for His glory.

This study is inductive, which simply means that three questions will undergird our exploration of Paul's letter: What does it say? What does it mean? and How does it apply to my life? To help us answer these questions, the lessons include critical historical details, context and content explanations, key word tutorials, and relevant life application. Over the course of the study, you will read through Ephesians several times. But don't stress—the entire epistle easily can be read in one sitting in about fifteen minutes. Just think, most of us spend more than fifteen minutes scrolling through social media in one day! Once we grasp the big picture overview in Week 1, we will break Ephesians down into shorter sections in the remaining weeks, studying it verse by verse.

Though this is an in-depth study, covering all of Paul's letter, it is written to be accessible for anyone, whether you are seasoned in Bible study or new to God's Word. I hope the richness of this study excites and challenges you to know God more deeply and who you are in Him. As we take this journey together, my desire is that we will be awestruck by the beauty, majesty, and glory of God; that we will be undone with love for Jesus; and that we will overflow with gratitude as we behold the Father's incredible plan to redeem and restore us to Himself. This glorious plan, called the gospel, is perhaps most clearly taught and explained in Ephesians. My earnest prayer as we faithfully examine its words is that we are transformed into the masterpiece God intends us to be!

The Workbook

Within these pages you will find five days of lessons for each week of study. You will need

* a Bible in your favorite translation (or access to a Bible website),
* colored pens, pencils, or highlighters for marking key words in the Scripture (if desired), and
* about 30 minutes per day to complete each lesson.

In each lesson you'll find a "Focal Point" Scripture verse, questions and exercises for reflection and response, and space for writing a prayer to God. You'll also find additional insights in the margin, called "The Big Picture," offering background information, cultural or context details, word definitions, and more that will help fill in the gaps and give you the full view of Ephesians, so to speak. I urge you not to skip a single lesson, since each one builds upon the previous lesson to bring us to a glorious conclusion.

Although you may make your way through this workbook alone or as part of a group study, the benefits of meeting with a group weekly include encouragement, discussion, community, and accountability. Either way, this workbook is intended to be used in tandem with the video teachings, which will greatly enhance your study experience.

The Video Teachings

The teaching videos are available separately on DVD (wherever books are sold) or as individual streaming video files (www.Cokesbury.com).

Whether doing the study alone or with a group, you will watch the video teaching for each week *before* completing the homework for that week. If meeting with a group, this means you will have six weeks of study but seven group sessions together. A Video Viewer Guide that you may complete while watching the video is provided at the beginning of each week's lessons. Full session guides with discussion questions, activities, prayer suggestions, and other leader helps are available in a separate leader guide.

Let's Get Started!

My heart is about to burst as I ponder the power, love, and wisdom of God revealed in Ephesians. I'm thrilled you've decided to dive into God's Word with me over the next six weeks. The truths found in this epistle have radically transformed my life, and I pray they will do the same for you. We can only know who we are when we discover *Whose* we are; and you, dear one, are chosen and beloved by the King of glory!

As we embark on this journey, I want you to know I am praying for you. I pray you behold the glory of God and are filled with awe as you discover the heights and depths of God's love for you. Truly, our God is an incredible Artist, creating a beautiful masterpiece to display His glory!

For His Glory,

Marian

SESSION 1: VIDEO VIEWER GUIDE

Ephesians 1:1-2 – Get to know the Artist, God

Ephesians 1:3-14 (prologue) – Get to know the author, Paul

Key Verse: *Ephesians 1:13*

Gospel – news that brings _____

Bisser – a _____

Isaiah 61:1-3 – Jesus proclaims a new Kingdom of good news

Matthew 4:23 – Jesus' miracles prove He is the King who came to establish a new kingdom

Ephesians 3:7 – Paul declares himself a proclaimer of the gospel

"The gospel is good news that 'changes your
_____ forever.'" — Tim Keller

WEEK 1: PREPPING THE CANVAS

Overview

For His Glory . . . These three words are the heartbeat of Ephesians. They emanate the purpose for which God the Father moved heaven and earth to redeem those who trust in His Son, Jesus Christ. Before we dive into our verse-by-verse study of Ephesians, which has been called "the queen of the epistles," it is paramount that we understand the biblical and cultural background that this magnificent message is built upon. The context of this letter proves vital to grasping the life-changing truths that God longs to speak to our hearts.

This week we prepare the canvas by discovering the *who*, *what*, *when*, *where*, and most important, the *why* behind this letter to the church in Ephesus. We will get to know both the author and the recipients, as well as uncover the reason why God redeems us. It is a joy to travel this journey with you as we discover the depths of God's love and hear the Voice of Truth who declares us to be His masterpiece. I'm praying for you as you dive into God's word these next six weeks!

DAY 1: THE CANVAS

Focal Point

Begin today's study by reading Ephesians 2:10.

> For we are God's masterpiece. He has created us anew in Christ Jesus, so we can do the good things he planned for us long ago.
>
> *EPHESIANS 2:10 NLT*

Have you ever seen a street after a parade? The lonesome scraps and fragments that are left seem dirty, abandoned, and trashed. Run over. What a shift from the moment before when music trilled, drums beat, and colors burst before our eyes. What fun! What exhilaration! And then . . . it's gone. Confetti becomes litter, songs trail to silence. The thrill of the party is a fleeting memory and only debris is left, bound for a dumpster. This, my friend, is how I describe my life before Jesus—I partied hard, but in the end I felt like trash.

Praise God, Jesus is a great Redeemer. Redemption means to buy something back and restore it to its original intent. Jesus is in the restoration business. Like a master artist, He takes the broken and makes us beautiful—all for the glory of His great name.

I was in my mid-twenties when I first met my Redeemer and began learning the truths you hold in this study. Before that, I was a trashed party-girl, searching for love in all the wrong places. But then LOVE found me, and love's name is Jesus.

I heard the good news—that Jesus wanted to restore the broken pieces of my life and create a masterpiece. The Bible says, "If anyone is in Christ, he is a new creation. The old has passed away; behold, the new has come" (2 Corinthians 5:17). It seemed too good to be true that I could go from trash to treasure, but this transformation business is Jesus' specialty.

Hearing this good news, I ran hard after Him. I absolutely fell in love with the One who rescued me, forgave my sin, and offered me a new life. But here's the thing: although I was following Jesus, somewhere deep inside I still believed I was trash. The truth of my new identity had not traveled the ten inches from my head to my heart.

11

*Jesus is
in the
restoration
business.*

A powerful lie was lodged deep within, infecting my identity. No matter what Jesus had done for me and declared in His word, I still had a hard time believing God could ever love a girl like me. Although I was devoted to following Christ, I was operating out of a poisoned self-image. Then one beautiful night, amid a battle for my heart and mind, Jesus spoke these words: "Marian, you are not that girl anymore." Jesus, the Voice of Truth, declared:

> *You are loved.*
> *You are chosen.*
> *You are My masterpiece.*

Jesus said, "You will know the truth, and the truth will set you free" (John 8:32 NIV). Girls, today I *am* free! I know who I am because I know Whose I am. My prayer for this study is that the same would be true for you in the depths of your heart!

Since Ephesians declares that we are God's masterpiece, it is fitting that we take time before we dive into our verse-by-verse study to prep the canvas. Just as an artist prepares her pallet, brushes, and canvas before embarking on creating a piece of art, we too must prepare ourselves to study Ephesians. This week we will explore the *who, what, when, where,* and *why* of Ephesians. Today we begin with *what* and examine the behind-the-scenes battle that wages against God's people and why the Lord needs to rescue us.

Stolen Masterpieces

Perhaps no person in modern history is more villainous than Adolf Hitler, the infamous leader of the German Nazi party during World War II. Hitler's forces ruthlessly slaughtered millions of people on battlefields and in death camps. While numerous books and movies are devoted to this man, there is one aspect of his life and character not widely known: Hitler's love for art and his personal aspirations to be an artist.

As a young man, Hitler believed himself to be a gifted painter, and he applied to and was rejected by Vienna's Academy of Fine Arts. The rejection was deeply felt. When Hitler became chancellor of Germany, his love for art and desire for his own glory collided in a most devious scheme. He devised a plan to steal the world's great art pieces for himself and place them in a museum he planned to construct called the *Fuhrermuseum*, which he envisioned as a monument to himself. His vanity and lust for glory are on full display in the greatest art heist in the history of the world.

While Hitler was attempting to take over the Western world, his armies methodically hoarded the finest art treasures in Europe. They plundered every church, cathedral, synagogue, and home in between. Nazi soldiers confiscated the art and shipped it back to hidden bunkers in Germany. "In a race against time, behind enemy lines, a special force of American and British museum directors, curators, art historians, and others called the Monuments Men risked their lives scouring Europe to prevent the destruction of thousands of years of culture. These men and women sacrificed everything to discover and restore these masterpieces to their rightful owners."[1]

I first learned of this great art heist while watching the film *The Monuments Men*. Since then, I've read numerous books about Hitler's diabolical desire to amass the world's masterpieces for himself. While this story is intriguing on its own merit, it proves a powerful illustration to help us understand what some scholars suggest is one of the overarching message of Ephesians—that God rescues those who trust in Jesus Christ from captivity to Satan's schemes, sin, and shame and restores us as His glorious masterpiece.

To comprehend the depth of this rescue mission to redeem us, we must start with who God is. God, the Creator of all things visible and invisible, is the ultimate artist. He has no rival or equal. He is the inventor of color and light. From His imagination came forth the brilliance of stars, the splendor of a sunrise, the majesty of mountains, and the most pivotal of His creations, you—His image bearer. Like any artist, the work of His hands reflects His glory. To see God, first and foremost, as an artist who designs and creates masterpieces is fundamental to our study of Ephesians.

Let's begin by reading the Creation account found in Genesis 1:1-31. What do you discover about who God is in this text?

⁴What is man that you are mindful of him, and the son of man that you care for him? ⁵Yet you have made him a little lower than the heavenly beings and crowned him with glory and honor. ⁶You have given him dominion over the works of your hands; you have put all things under his feet.

PSALM 8:4-6

"The thief comes only to steal and kill and destroy. I came that they may have life and have it abundantly."

JOHN 10:10

What word did God use to describe His creation? "It was _____" (vv. 10, 12, 18, 21, 25, 31).

What do you discover about humanity in Genesis 1:26-27? In whose image are we created?

The Bible elevates humanity above any other created being because we are made in God's image. To bear God's image does not mean that we are gods; rather, it means we are distinct from animals and similar to God in our mental, moral, and social capabilities.

Read Psalm 8:4-6 in the margin. According to this psalm, with what is humanity crowned?

Before we dig into Ephesians, we must understand that Scripture reveals there is an enemy who despises God's glory and opposes us, God's glorious image bearers. Just as Hitler lusted after the great masterpieces of the world for his own fame, our enemy seeks to take us captive, in a manner of speaking, for his own purposes and agenda. This enemy, who is referenced in Scripture by various names—including Satan, devil, accuser, adversary, tempter, and others—is opposed to anyone who glorifies the ultimate Artist. Jesus himself defined our enemy's purpose and agenda.

Read John 10:10 in the margin. Jesus described the enemy as a "thief." What does the thief come to do?

The thief comes to _____ and _____ and _____.

What did Jesus come to give us?

Like Hitler, who tried to amass the world's art for himself, our enemy seeks to take captive humanity for his own devious purposes.

Though we will be focusing on God, rather than our enemy, throughout this study, understanding Satan's agenda to steal, kill, and destroy is fundamental to understanding our own stories and unlocking the beautiful truths found in Ephesians. This brings us to our backstory.

Our Backstory

Human beings are hardwired to live in relationship with God. But we were not created as robots, we've been given free will, which means we can freely choose who or what we will love and worship. Before sin entered the world, Adam and Eve enjoyed intimate community with God. All of their needs for significance and belonging were met in Him. Life was free from heartache, insecurity, and pain. Oneness with God was our intended design. So what happened? How did we fall so far?

First of all, we must note that God gave Adam specific instructions about life in the garden.

Read Genesis 2:15-17 in the margin. Adam is given freedom to eat from all the trees found in the garden but one. From which tree is he instructed not to eat?

In Genesis 3, we discover how humanity chose to disobey God, ushering in sin and the destruction that resulted from it; the moment when we lost connection with our Life-source.

Read Genesis 3 and answer the following:
How did the serpent tempt Eve? (vv. 1-4)

What did the serpent accuse God of withholding from Adam and Eve? (v. 5)

¹⁵The LORD God took the man and put him in the Garden of Eden to work it and take care of it. ¹⁶And the LORD God commanded the man, "You are free to eat from any tree in the garden; ¹⁷but you must not eat from the tree of the knowledge of good and evil, for when you eat from it you will certainly die."
GENESIS 2:15-17 NIV

The Big Picture

One source defines sin as "actions by which humans rebel against God, miss his purpose for their lives, and surrender to the power of evil."[2] Sin can be active rebellion or passive indifference; either way, it is falling short of the glory of God for which we were created to reflect to the world.

What were Adam and Eve's first reactions after taking of the forbidden fruit? (vv. 8-13)

How did God respond to their rebellion? (v. 21)

Where were Adam and Eve sent because they believed the serpent's lies? (vv. 22-24)

The serpent suggested that they could become autonomous and decide what is true for themselves. In this moment of rebellion, connection with our Creator was shattered and life as God intended for us was marred by sin. Adam and Eve hid from God (shame) and straightaway began to point the finger at each other (blame). This fallen nature, called sin, was transmitted to every human being born outside the garden of Eden (see Romans 5:11-21). Apart from Christ, we all have this sinful nature, and it is the source of all hate, insecurity, fear, shame, guilt, pain, and brokenness we experience.

In the Bible we read,

> *All have sinned and fall short of the glory of God.*
> ROMANS 3:23

> *There is a way that seems right to a man, but its end is the way to death.*
> PROVERBS 16:25

> *The wages of sin is death, but the free gift of God is eternal life in Christ Jesus our Lord.*
> ROMANS 6:23

It proves difficult for us to imagine a world free of sin, selfishness, sorrow, and death. A broken world is all we've known, but this is not God's original design. All of this heartache resulted from the fall of humanity.

How have you personally tasted of the destruction of sin and the devastation it brings to God's image bearers?

Before Jesus rescued me, I was a broken young woman. My life was riddled by the effects of sin done to me, but also by my own choices to rebel against God. I look back on my redemption story and see fingerprints of grace and the work of the Master to create a masterpiece. Therefore, I close today with the good news. While it is true that humanity has fallen short of the glory of God and we fight against an enemy whose primary agenda is our destruction, we rejoice that God's ultimate plan for fellowship with us was not thwarted. *The entire Epistle of Ephesians tells of the rescue mission that God initiated and completed in His Son, Jesus Christ, and this will be our focus throughout our study together.* We are about to embark on a journey to see the supreme wisdom, power, and love of God displayed in a plan so magnificent that it leaves the angels breathless in wonder and humanity gloriously redeemed. Friend, I can't help fast forwarding to the end of this story and celebrate with you the best news of all time—Jesus wins!

The entire epistle of Ephesians tells of the rescue mission that God initiated and completed in His Son, Jesus Christ.

Prayer

In the space below, connect with God using your own words:

DAY 2: FOR THE PRAISE OF HIS GLORY

Focal Point

Begin today's study by reading Ephesians 1:3-6.

In 2009, Simon Sinek gave a TED talk titled "Start with Why," which went on to become one of the most popular TED talks of all time. What was so revolutionary about this talk? I think it resonated with millions because it boiled down human behavior and business success to the simple question "Why?" Sinek's basic principle is this: What you do is not nearly as important as why you do it.

Our goal this week is to prep the canvas and lay the foundation for our study of Ephesians. We will discover the context for this God-breathed letter that has transformed countless lives for all eternity. But before we can proceed into the depths, we need to step back and ask the all-important question: *Why?*

God's Why

Let's begin by examining today's Focal Point, which we will unpack more fully next week. These verses offer praise to God the Father for how He has blessed us in Christ Jesus. Verses 5-6 prove an important key to unlocking the why behind God's plan to redeem us.

Read verse 5 and fill in the blanks: "According to the _____ of his _____."

Now write verse 6:
"to the praise of _____."

Verse 6 is a powerful hint at God's why. Tuck that word *glorious* into your pocket as we continue our study.

Why proves to be a crucial question. This simple three-letter word gives understanding to someone's purpose, motives, and values. We get insight into God's *why* in Jesus' prayer in the garden of Gethsemane the night before His death. In this intimate conversation between Father and Son, we learn of the primary motivation behind Jesus' ministry and sacrificial death.

Read John 17:1-5.

What is Jesus' motivation? (v. 1)

What does Jesus give to those who believe in Him? (v. 2)

How is eternal life defined? (v. 3)

How did Jesus bring the Father glory? (v. 4)

Glory is God's *why*! He orchestrated a divine plan to restore a lost humanity to Himself for one magnificent reason—to showcase His glory to the world. It is through this rescue mission, which we call the gospel, that God's heart is most clearly revealed. Through redemption, love is defined. Through the gospel, we discover a Father who pursues us in order to reconcile us. Through all that God did to make us right with Him, we behold His glory, which is the purpose for which Jesus entered the human story. As John's Gospel declares concerning Jesus, "The Word became flesh and dwelt among us, and we have seen his glory, glory as of the only Son from the Father, full of grace and truth" (John 1:14).

Lean into those two marvelous words—*grace* and *truth*. Each of us thirsts for the life that can only be experienced through the grace of God, but we also hunger for truth that sets us free. In Jesus, who

Redemption is God's specialty and the heartbeat of Ephesians.

reveals the glory of God, we experience both. We start with *why* today so that we can understand the driving passion of God the Father to reveal His love, grace, truth, justice, holiness, and wisdom through His Son, Jesus Christ.

Yesterday we discovered that the Lord God Almighty is the brilliant Creator of all things and that we human beings are created in His image. We also learned that we have an enemy who seeks to kill, steal, and destroy. Understanding our beautiful design and who we are as God's masterpiece is the basis for all we will explore together. This starting point explains *why* we were created and our tragic fall from glory that required Jesus to die for our redemption.

Without jumping too far ahead in our study, I want to pause and share with you my love for the word *redemption*. After all, I call myself a Redeemed Girl. As we saw yesterday, *redeemed* means to buy something back and to restore it to its original intent. This word is infused with images of restoration, new life, and transformation. Just think of some of our favorite television shows like *Fixer Upper* on HGTV. Redemption is the heart behind these programs. The broken is made beautiful. Something abandoned, unwanted, and trashed is gloriously rescued and restored. I firmly believe that these television shows resonate with our hearts because we all long for restoration too. Friend, redemption is God's specialty and the heartbeat of Ephesians.

In what ways has your life been like an episode of a home renovation show?

How have you personally experienced God's redemptive power?

The old saying goes, "The art reveals the artist." This adage proves true when we think of God's heart and motive for redemption. While today's study will not unpack all that redemption is (that will come next week), I do want to establish God's primary motivation for redemption—to restore us to a loving relationship with Himself, which magnifies His greatness and brings glory to His name. The

Bible makes it clear that the chief aim of Jesus' sacrificial death and resurrection is to display His glory to the world. The Lord was under no obligation to rescue humanity from the destruction of sin, but as Ephesians will make abundantly clear, He did! God's divine attributes of holiness, love, and justice are most clearly revealed in the work of salvation. And as we will discover in Ephesians, redemption was accomplished for "the praise of His Glory."

God's Glory Displayed

To begin, let's explore further how God's glory is displayed through His creation. This is called general revelation, which means that all people can know there is a God by observing what He created.

Read Psalm 19:1-4. What does the creation do according to these verses?

What can someone learn about God's nature (character, power, personality) by simply observing the vastness of space, or an ocean teeming with life, or a spectacular sunrise?

Throughout the Bible, God's glory is on display and is the primary motivation for all His deeds, so that we might know His heart. It was *for His glory* that He delivered His people from slavery in Egypt. It was the glory of God that filled the temple in Jerusalem, where God's people worshiped Him. It is the radiance of God's glory that Jesus revealed when He stepped into the human story to serve as our Savior (John 1:14).

Read the following Scriptures describing God's glory (His nature and character), and record what you observe in response to the following prompts:

The Big Picture
Glory is the public display of the infinite beauty and immeasurable worth of God. Glory is all of His divine attributes (His love, holiness, truth, justice, omniscience, omnipotence, goodness, and power) revealed. Glory is God's radiant perfection made known.[3]

21

2 Chronicles 7:1-3—Note what occurred when God's glory was revealed in the temple:

Psalm 145—Note how the psalmist praises God's glorious nature:

Hebrews 1:1-3—Note who is the radiance of God's glory:

Friend, the Bible is one story, comprising sixty-six different books, written over a span of two thousand years by numerous human authors inspired by the Holy Spirit. These individual books work in tandem to tell the one glorious story of redemption. The grand narrative of the Bible is God's plan to rescue humanity from sin and to adopt us into His family. Ephesians is one of the clearest explanations of God's work to redeem us so that we might know His love and live for His glory.

Understanding the Big Picture

Our primary goal today is to read all of Ephesians in one sitting. In ancient times, epistles were read aloud to a group and the entire scope of the communication would have been received at one time. So, I want you to experience the heart of this letter and allow the message to unfold just as the original recipients would have first heard it. Today's study is all about understanding the big picture— the glory of God!

Turn in your Bible to Ephesians and read chapters 1–6. If you are comfortable marking in your Bible, mark the following words or terms with a yellow or gold pen or highlighter as you read:

| God | Glory | Glorify | Glorious |

Take your time. Savor each word of Ephesians as if it were a letter written directly to you. Read slowly and thoughtfully. Before you begin, prayerfully ask the Holy Spirit to illuminate His word and highlight truths that are for you specifically today.

What did you glean from your reading?

What verse(s) jumped off the page as you carefully pored over God's word?

What did you learn about the glory of God?

> God is pursuing you so that His glory can be displayed through you, His masterpiece.

As we wrap up Day 2 of our study, we've covered a key concept to help us understand Ephesians—God's motivation for redemption. As we look at Jesus, we see God is full of grace and truth. This means that He is for you and not against you. This means that God is pursuing you so that His glory can be displayed through you, His masterpiece. I'm so proud of you for the time you've invested in digging into Scripture and for allowing the Holy Spirit to reveal truth to your heart.

Prayer

In the space below, connect with God using your own words:

DAY 3: PAUL, THE APOSTLE

Focal Point

Begin today's study by reading Ephesians 1:1.

As a mom of three, I spend more time than I care to admit in the grocery store. This task proves challenging with a two-year-old who screams for ice cream while momma shops for ground beef. Like most moms, I've discovered ways to entertain her while I debate important purchase decisions such as asparagus or broccoli. Yes, I confess, I sometimes cave and do what I swore up and down I'd never do—hand her my phone so she can play while I shop in peace.

Yesterday an older woman stopped me and marveled at my daughter, Sydney. She watched my toddler effortlessly maneuver my smartphone. Sydney flipped back and forth between her favorite cartoon and the music app with ease. The woman was astounded that a device still so foreign to her is a familiar world to my daughter. She stated how much communication has transformed in her lifetime. Even though I am half her age, I wholeheartedly agree; personal communication has changed drastically. Today . . .

- Handwritten letters are a relic of the past and are now called "snail mail."
- Loved ones separated by oceans no longer wait for months to see one another; they easily connect within seconds via video chat.
- Relationships often start, stop, and stay connected via text messages.

In the modern communication age, we convey our thoughts to others through a variety of means. This was not the case in the day in which Ephesians was penned. In the ancient Roman world, if one desired to communicate with someone in a different city or foreign land, there was only one method available, and that was to send a letter, or what was known as an epistle.

Paul's Letter

In my office is an old trunk filled with handwritten letters dating all the way back to my days in elementary school. Some evoke strong emotions as I see the handwriting of loved ones who've passed away. Others make me laugh at the girl I once was and my eye-roll-worthy high school drama. However, there is one note I'll always treasure because I received it at a particularly low point in my life. As a teenager, I was riddled with insecurity and shame, and my camp counselor sent me a letter telling me how much she hoped to have a daughter like me one day. Up until that moment, I had believed every lie Satan had thrown at me about my value and worth and couldn't believe anyone would want a girl like me. That letter was a gift from God and a ray of light during an extremely dark season.

What is the most meaningful letter you've ever received? Why?

Ephesians was a letter sent to the church to convey important doctrinal truths—central beliefs—and to encourage the believers in their faith. As you read this letter you can hear the passion of the sender and how deeply he wants the ones who read it to grasp the significance of the truth he shares. One thing has not changed through the centuries: identifying the sender and the recipient of a letter is essential to understanding that letter. This fact leads us to our goal for today. Before we can dive into the meat of this message, we need to get to know who is sending this epistle and to whom he is writing.

Read Ephesians 1:1-2 and answer the following:

Who is the sender or author of the epistle? What title does he use to describe himself?

The Big Picture

*The word **epistle** simply means a letter. James Montgomery Boice writes, "Ephesians was originally composed as a circular letter intended for all the seven churches of Asia—those established by Paul or his followers during the time of his ministry in Ephesus—and that the name Ephesus became identified with the epistle because it was the chief city [in the region]."[4]*

25

The Big Picture

*The word **apostle** describes a distinctive group among the disciples whom Jesus designated to take His gospel to the world and then establish churches. Only those who were eyewitness to His resurrection were qualified to be apostles (Acts 1:21-22). "Paul qualified because he had seen the risen Christ (1 Corinthians 15:4-10)."[5]*

Read the Extra Insight in the margin. How does the title "apostle" give Paul more credibility?

The apostle Paul opens his letter to the Ephesians by clearly identifying himself and stating his position of authority. To fully appreciate this man used by God to pen this incredible letter to the church, we need to know his redemption story.

Transformed by Christ

I love transformation stories! One of my favorite movies depicts a radical transformation. Long before Gwyneth Paltrow became famous for her role in *The Avengers*, she starred in a movie in the late 1990s called *Sliding Doors*. In the film, Paltrow's character is forever altered by the mere sliding of a subway door, which causes her to miss a train. The film reveals how her life would have proceeded had she walked through that door, making the train—and it shows in parallel what occurs because she didn't walk through the door. The two storylines play out side by side on the silver screen.

The thought that one decision could alter the destiny of one's life forever is a fascinating concept, isn't it? Coincidentally, it was around the time I first watched this movie that my own life headed down a radically different path. What was the event that caused such a trajectory shift? It was when Jesus reached into my darkness and, by grace, rescued me:

> [13]*For he [God] has rescued us from the dominion of darkness and brought us into the kingdom of the Son he loves, *[14]*in whom we have redemption, the forgiveness of sins.*
> COLOSSIANS 1:13-14 NIV

Sitting in a bar, looking for love in all the wrong places, I cried out to God for help. (Yes, God hears us wherever we are—even in a bar!) A few weeks later, a friend invited me to her church, where I heard about the gospel and how Jesus could set me free from my sin and give me new life. Before Jesus, I was in a downward spiral of destruction. Thankfully, God's grace intersected my hot mess, setting me free and putting me on a path to freedom. Jesus said,

> ⁹"I am the door. If anyone enters by me, he will be saved and will go in and out and find pasture. ¹⁰The thief comes only to steal and kill and destroy. I came that they may have life and have it abundantly."
>
> JOHN 10:9-10

I find it profound that Jesus described Himself as "the door." A door is an entry point. Jesus is the way back into fellowship with God. All of humanity stands outside this door, and we must choose whether or not we will enter through the door by grace and experience the abundant life God has for us.

On Day 1 we looked at how sin entered the world (Genesis 3) and how Adam and Eve were expelled from the garden of Eden. From that moment forward, God, our heavenly Father, had a plan to redeem humanity and make a way for us to come back into a loving relationship with Him. The way back is through Jesus Christ, the door. This is a door opened by grace, which we will marvel at in depth throughout our study.

How does the image of Jesus as the door in John 10:9-10 shed light on your understanding of God's glorious plan of redemption?

As a twenty-five-year-old woman, I stood at this door. On one side was the world of rebellion and emptiness I'd known; on the other side was surrender to a Savior and a promise of real life. By my faith and God's grace, I stepped through Jesus, the door, and my life has never been the same. Initially, I understood I was forgiven. And over time, I began to see evidence of the abundant life Jesus promised. What I've come to understand after nearly two decades of this redeemed life is this: **Jesus didn't just save me *from* my sins; Jesus freed me *for* the incredible life my heavenly Father destined for me.**

Jesus is the way back into fellowship with God.

Honestly, I shudder to think where I would have ended up had I not walked through the door. What if I had continued in my self-destructive ways? I would not have been healed from my childhood wounds and come to know the fullness of abundant life in Christ. I would not have married the amazing man God had planned for me. I would not be raising godly children. And I sure wouldn't be preaching the Word. Though Satan had a plan to destroy me, he has no power against the God who redeemed me!

The apostle Paul has his own transformation story to tell. His story is told in detail multiple times in the Book of Acts. Let's begin by looking at the first account of the event that turned him from a persecutor of Christians to a proclaimer of Christ. As we read this account, it is important to note that previously Paul, also known as Saul, witnessed and consented to the execution of Stephen, a devout follower of Jesus (see Acts 7:54-60). The Bible doesn't hide Saul's sin. He was a religious zealot who hunted down Jesus' followers, casting them into prison and mercilessly persecuting them. Let's turn our focus to God's Word and behold how Jesus can take anyone and transform that person into a masterpiece for His glory.

Read the first account of Saul's conversion as told in Acts 9 and answer the following:

Why was Saul traveling to Damascus? (vv. 1-2)

Whom did he encounter on the way? (vv. 3-7)

What happened to Saul as a result of this encounter? (vv. 7-8)

How was Saul's sight restored? (vv. 10-18)

What did Saul immediately begin to do in Damascus? (vv. 20-22)

In Acts 26, Paul testifies before King Agrippa. Many years have passed since his transformation, and now Paul is a prisoner on trial for his life. It is in this setting that he sheds greater light on his background and the dramatic encounter with Christ that transformed him.

Read Acts 26:1-29 and record what you learn about the apostle Paul by answering the following:

How did Paul describe his life before he met Jesus on the road to Damascus?

What further details did he provide about his encounter with Christ?

> *Only when we are aware of our own brokenness do we recognize our need for God's supernatural work of restoration.*

Saul's companions were stricken with terror. Lying flat upon the dirt, Saul heard the words that were spoken and saw clearly before him Jesus, the Son of God. No doubt Jesus' words sliced through any arguments like a sword, flooding the darkened chambers of Saul's mind with light and revealing the astonishing truth. He now realized that, although he imagined himself to be zealously serving God by persecuting the followers of Christ, he actually was opposing the One true God—Jesus Christ.

According to Acts 26:15-18, what did Jesus appoint Paul to do?

Thinking back to what we've learned so far in our study, how does the apostle Paul's calling fit into God's plan to redeem humanity?

Saul was transformed from a ruthless, hateful man into the apostle Paul, who penned most of the New Testament and spread God's love across the globe. It was the brilliant light of Jesus' glory that knocked Saul off his horse, searing his heart with a deep awareness of his own sin. This illumination was the beginning of Saul's transformation, and it proves to be the beginning of each of ours. For only when we are aware of our own brokenness do we recognize our need for God's supernatural work of restoration. Like Saul, most of us need to be "knocked off our high horse" of self-importance to realize that the One to whom all glory is due is the same One who came to save our souls.

Thinking back on my own faith journey, I know it was God's grace that intervened in my life, showing me my sin and my desperate need for Christ, my Savior. I was busy living for myself, searching for love in all the wrong places, and pretending I was fine. But the reality is that I was actually desperate for God. I'm thankful that God's glorious light breaks through our darkness, illuminating the path called *grace*. Paul's story reminds us that no one is beyond the grace of God. Jesus can take the hardest heart and transform it for His glory!

Prayer

In the space below, connect with God using your own words:

DAY 4: TO THE SAINTS WHO ARE IN EPHESUS

Focal Point

Begin today's study by reading Ephesians 1:1-2.

Back when I was a young, single woman—before getting married, becoming a stepmom to two incredible boys, and amazingly having a daughter of my own in my early forties—I had copious amounts of free time. Honestly, I didn't realize how precious the gift of time was until my days became dictated by nap schedules, the school tardy bell, and after-school activities. During my single-girl days, I spent much of my free time traveling the globe with my girlfriends—thanks to the fact that I was a schoolteacher who had summers off and could easily indulge my passion for travel.

Why did I love to travel so much? For starters, I'm a history nut. Traveling is a way of exploring antiquity and soaking in various cultures—not to mention my penchant for a good cup of coffee and a buttery croissant. No one, and I repeat no one, does pastry like the French! *God bless 'em!* I digress. I could talk about French pastries far too long. There's one thing I love more than the food when I travel, and that's an excellent tour guide. I want someone who knows the area to give me background scoop on whatever castle, cathedral, or city I'm exploring. Frankly, a large stone monument is just a piece of sandstone until someone with knowledge explains the fascinating facts behind Stonehenge. A guide is a good thing! Also, should you ever visit my hometown of San Antonio, Texas, rest assured, I would teach you all about the Alamo and Texas history. Honestly, I can't help myself, but we would substitute the pastries with some good ol' chips and queso!

I want to take the next few minutes to serve as your official tour guide to the ancient city of Ephesus. Why? If we are to appreciate the letter written to the church in this area, it is helpful to understand something of the culture of the day. While the words of

The Big Picture

Artemis: *"Ephesus was the center of the cult of Artemis. . . . [I]n the ancient metropolis of Ephesus, Artemis symbolized sexual fertility. The idols that represent Artemis and have been found today show a rather grotesque, multi-breasted female figure. In Ephesus, as in other Greek and Roman temples, a great deal of the so-called worship of the goddess was actually cult prostitution. Sex worship had a hold on the people, as it does on many of our contemporaries though in a different form. Their condition was typical of the world at the time of Christ."[7]*

Ephesians are the breath of God for all generations, we can't ignore the fact that the Holy Spirit chose a particular city and context for a specific purpose to reveal divine truth. As we continue this week to prep the canvas for our study, we must pause to ask the question—*where?* Understanding more about Ephesus, the region where this letter was sent, will greatly help us appreciate the riches found within it.

In the ancient world, Ephesus was a hub of travel and commerce. Situated on the coast of the Aegean Sea at the mouth of the Cayster River, the city was one of the most significant seaports of the ancient world, considered second largest in population after the capital city of Rome.

Ephesus was an ancient port city in modern-day Turkey. The city was once considered the most important trading center in the Mediterranean region. The city was ruled by many powerful empires through the ages, including the Greek, Persian, Roman, Byzantine and Ottoman empires. Rich in culture and commerce, Ephesus remained a thriving city for generations. As one writer says:

> Ephesus' greatest claim to fame was its temple to the goddess Artemis. One of the "seven wonders" of the ancient world, it was almost four times larger than the Parthenon in Athens. According to the New Testament, the apostle Paul preached in Ephesus, prompting a riot led by silversmiths who crafted shrines to the goddess and feared for both their livelihoods and the future of the temple.[6]

We could compare Ephesus to any thriving contemporary city with a variety of cultures calling it home. Travelers from across the world descended upon Ephesus. I'd compare ancient Ephesus to modern-day New York City or Houston, Texas. Both are melting pots of cultures built around bustling seaports, welcoming commerce and travelers from across the globe.

Now that we know a little more about this ancient city, let's turn our attention to the Bible and learn of the apostle Paul's experiences in this region and with the church to whom he sent this epistle.

To review, read Acts 26:15-18 in the margin and answer the following:

What did Jesus send Paul to do? (vv. 16, 18)

What were those who believed Paul's message to receive? (v. 18)

Paul immediately began to proclaim Jesus as the long-awaited Messiah and Savior of the world (Acts 9:20). The Book of Acts records three missionary journeys Paul took throughout the Roman Empire in one of the greatest evangelistic endeavors in history. Paul was obedient to Jesus' call to be His witness and proclaim the gospel. He first ministered in Ephesus (approximately AD 53) but did not remain there (Acts 18:19-21). Two years later, while on his third missionary journey, Paul stayed in Ephesus for at least two years and shared Christ with the entire region (Acts 19:1-20). During these years, he founded a strong church in this city that was a major commercial hub in the region and attracted many visitors, since Ephesus was a religious center dedicated to the worship of the goddess Artemis.

To better understand Paul's ministry in Ephesus, let's take a few minutes to read the historical account of Paul's ministry there, which is found in Acts 19 and 20.

Begin by reading Acts 19:1-20. How long did Paul teach about the kingdom of God in Ephesus? (v. 10)

What was the result of Paul's teaching? (vv. 10-11)

How did those who practiced sorcery and magic in Ephesus demonstrate they were turning from evil and trusting in Jesus as Lord? (vv. 18-20)

[15]"And I [Paul] said, 'Who are you, Lord?' And the Lord said, 'I am Jesus whom you are persecuting. [16]But rise and stand upon your feet, for I have appeared to you for this purpose, to appoint you as a servant and witness to the things in which you have seen me and to those in which I will appear to you, [17]delivering you from your people and from the Gentiles—to whom I am sending you [18]to open their eyes, so that they may turn from darkness to light and from the power of Satan to God, that they may receive forgiveness of sins and a place among those who are sanctified by faith in me.'"

ACTS 26:15-18

The Big Picture

Paul had one consistent method as he traveled on his missionary journeys: He went into the local synagogue and taught from the Scriptures that Jesus was the long-awaited Messiah. As James Montgomery Boice writes, "He taught that this one, who had come in his own lifetime, who had lived, taught, died, and then been raised from the dead, this Jesus of Nazareth, was the fulfillment of the Old Testament Scriptures. He took the Old Testament, showed what God had said his Messiah would do, and then told how Jesus had done it."[8]

It proves hard for us to imagine a world in which sorcery was so common that those coming to Christ literally burned their objects of witchcraft as a symbol of their life change. What would be a modern-day equivalent for someone coming to Christ in our culture today? What is a sinful practice a person might turn away from when turning to Christ as their Lord?

Scripture teaches us that Paul preached in Ephesus for two years with immense response to his message. As a result of Paul's teaching, those who believed experienced genuine life change, just as Jesus told Paul they would—they turned from darkness to light. As a result of this massive transformation, even the local economy was affected! Why? Those who once worshiped the pagan goddess Artemis stopped their idolatry and put their hope and faith in the one true God—Jesus Christ. As one of my favorite commentators writes, "These Christians had come under the power of the Spirit of God through the preaching of the Word so thoroughly that they were convicted of sin, confessed it, and then actually brought out and destroyed the things that were opposed to Christianity."[9]

Due to this city-wide repentance, the local silversmiths became furious at the apostle Paul, the one who had brought the news of Jesus to the city of Ephesus. The details of this uproar are also found in Acts 19. Let's continue reading and discover the rest of the story.

Read Acts 19:23-41 and answer the following:

What did Demetrius the silversmith accuse Paul of doing? (vv. 23-28)

Many people took to the streets to protest, and many didn't even know why they were rioting (v. 32). What does this scene suggest about the culture of that day and the power of darkness, which didn't like Paul's preaching one bit? (vv. 29-41)

Recall that Jesus sent Paul to preach so that people could turn from the power of Satan to the power of God (Acts 26:18). We see the fruit of his ministry in Ephesus. Why do you think the darkness would oppose Paul's preaching?

The closing scene in Paul's relationship with the church at Ephesus is a poignant one. After the uproar with the silversmiths ended, Paul continued his travels to other areas en route to Jerusalem. In the next section of Acts 20, we find the apostle Paul meeting with leaders from the church in Ephesus. This touching goodbye tells us much about the affection Paul felt for the church in this city and the devotion the leaders felt for this beloved apostle.

Read Acts 20:17-37 and then answer the following questions:

What did Paul say he taught the people in Ephesus? (vv. 20-21)

What did Paul believe was awaiting him in the near future? (v. 23)

Did Paul expect to see these believers again? (v. 25)

What was Paul concerned would happen to this church after his departure? (vv. 29-31)

How do you think Paul felt leaving this church in which he had invested two years of his life teaching about Jesus?

As a result of Paul's teaching, those who believed experienced genuine life change . . . they turned from darkness to light.

35

Describe the emotional scene that happened at Paul's leaving. How do you think the leaders felt about this man? (vv. 36-37)

We've spent the greater part of our study today getting acquainted with the apostle Paul's relationship with the church in Ephesus. As we've discovered, Paul was extremely devoted to this beloved church. His sense of protection for them was due to a fatherly concern for their well-being. Just imagine the anguish the church felt at Paul's departure, especially knowing that hardship and persecution awaited him.

Today we've gleaned a great deal from this behind-the-scenes look at the saints in Ephesus. As we dive into our verse-by-verse study next week, I hope you'll read each word remembering the deep love and devotion Paul felt for this church and his desire for them to hold fast to Jesus. That same desire reaches through the ages and through Paul's writing to touch us today. Just think . . . these words that were inspired by the Holy Spirit are meant for you and me! Ephesians empowers, encourages, and equips us to live for God's glory!

Prayer

In the space below, connect with God using your own words:

DAY 5: FAITHFUL IN CHRIST JESUS

Focal Point

Begin today's study by reading Ephesians 1:1-2.

Jesus' plan to transform the world and rescue humanity involved a simple strategy: discipleship. Discipleship is the act of one person teaching another how to know God personally and walk in His truth. It's important to note that the word *disciple* also conveys someone who is wholeheartedly committed to following Jesus. In Matthew 28:18-20, what is known as the Great Commission, Jesus told His followers to go into all the world and make disciples. As we've discovered in the past few days, the apostle Paul was faithful to that call. If you are a Christ-follower today, you and I can trace our spiritual heritage all the way back to the ministry of Paul.

Recently the woman who discipled me came to my home in San Antonio for a quick visit. She's more than just a friend; she's my spiritual mentor. When we are together, we do the things many women like to do—we shop, we eat, we watch movies. But because our friendship is built on Jesus, we talk primarily about what God is doing in our lives. She was the person God used to teach me His word, prayerfully guide me during major life decisions, and encourage me when I was stepping out into ministry. When I'm with my friend, I can imagine how the church at Ephesus felt about Paul. He faithfully taught them God's word, fought for them in prayer, and trained the leaders of this young church.

Who has God used to help grow and establish your faith in Jesus? Who has been like the apostle Paul in your spiritual journey, and how has this person impacted your life?

For to me to live
is Christ, and to
die is gain.
PHILIPPIANS 1:21

Paul traversed the Roman Empire, making disciples and telling both Jews and Gentiles (more on those terms in coming days) that Jesus is the hope of humanity and Savior of the world. His heart for the world to know Christ fueled every step of his missionary journeys and kept him pressing on even when facing harsh critics, religious persecution, and outright spiritual warfare. One word that springs to mind when I think of this faithful servant is *passion*. Paul possessed an incomparable zeal for Jesus.

Read Philippians 1:21 in the margin, Paul's personal mission statement. What was his purpose for living?

Now It's your turn. What is your life purpose? In other words, what fuels your life and gives meaning to your day?

Every word of the epistle we are studying bursts forth from the heart of a man who is consumed with the glory of God. His motivation in life is to lift high the name of Jesus and for the world to know life in Him. Paul had been a Christian for nearly thirty years by the time he wrote Ephesians. He had established churches all around the Mediterranean Sea during his three missionary trips. Toward the end of the third missionary journey, he was arrested in the city of Jerusalem for causing a riot due to his preaching. Paul was determined to go to Rome (Acts 19:21), where God had told him he would go to preach the gospel (Acts 23:11). After being arrested, Paul appealed to Caesar and eventually did make it to Rome.

While there, Paul was under house arrest, and people from all over the Roman Empire made their way to the eternal city. As one source notes, "Though a prisoner, Paul was free to have visitors and to write letters. . . . Those who heard the gospel could take it, for Paul, to the ends of the earth."[10]

Clearly Paul's ministry was not hindered by his circumstances. While a prisoner in Rome he wrote many of the New Testament epistles, including Ephesians. But why did he write this letter? After all, he'd spent nearly three years there establishing the church and teaching them about Jesus. *What more did they need to know?* His motivation for the letter is found in his parting words to his beloved friends: "I know that after I leave, savage wolves will come in among you and will not spare the flock. Even from your own number men will arise and *distort the truth* in order to draw away disciples after them. So be on your guard!" (Acts 20:29-31a NIV, emphasis added).

We glean a little behind-the-scenes insight into what was happening in Ephesus after Paul's departure through his letter to Timothy, whom he left to oversee the church in Ephesus.

Read 1 Timothy 1:3-7. What do you think Paul is concerned will happen to his beloved church in Ephesus?

The language used here is vivid. What do you imagine a savage wolf would do to a lamb?

Paul knew young believers would be easy prey for false teachers. He feared the "savage wolves" would ravage the flock. So Paul wrote to remind the flock of the essential truths of the Christian faith so that the false teachers could not distort it and divide the church.

Our goal today is to read all of Ephesians 1-6 in one sitting. Each time we do this, we gain a better understanding of the big picture of this epistle. Before you begin, prayerfully ask the Holy Spirit to illuminate His word and highlight truths that are specifically for you today.

If you are comfortable marking in your Bible, mark the following references to the recipients with a blue highlighter or pen:

> *Saints*   *you*   *yours*   *us*   *we*

What did you discover in this second reading of Ephesians?

What did you learn about Paul's heart for the recipients of this letter?

Friend, I hope you've enjoyed our tour of the ancient city of Ephesus and getting acquainted with the apostle Paul. As we've prepped the canvas for our study, we've discovered the what (the battle against the souls of humanity), the why (the glory of God), the who (the believers in Ephesus), and the where (a bustling seaport city filled with people from diverse cultures and backgrounds). Next week we begin our verse-by-verse study of this glorious letter. I pray your heart is prepared to discover the rich inheritance God has for you in Christ Jesus!

Prayer

In the space below, connect with God using your own words:

Ephesians 1:11-12 – Our hope is in Christ

1. Paul talks about _____.

2. We are _____.

Ephesians 1:4 – We are chosen by God before creation

Ephesians 1:7 – We have redemption and forgiveness through Jesus' blood

2 Corinthians 5:17 – We are a new creation in Christ

2 Corinthians 5:21 – What is true of Jesus is true of you

3. The third important concept is the word _____.

Ephesians 1:12 – Our redemption story glorifies God

WEEK 2: THE GLORIOUS GOSPEL

Overview

This week we dive into the prologue of Ephesians in chapter 1 and discover how each person of the Holy Trinity—Father, Son, and Spirit—is intimately and actively involved in the glorious plan to redeem and restore us as God's masterpiece. Paul begins this epistle with rapturous praise to God the Father for the brilliance, majesty, and the perfection of His design to save us and to adopt us into His very own family. He then shifts his gaze to behold the love of Jesus, who sacrificially died to redeem us. Finally, he praises the Holy Spirit who is the sign and seal of our inheritance. As we walk verse by verse through this chapter, we will behold our rich inheritance in Christ and the spiritual blessings He accomplished for us. We will conclude on Day 5 by taking a close look at Paul's prayer for us to experience victory by accessing Jesus' resurrection power in our daily lives. The truths in Ephesians are absolutely life-changing. I'm thrilled to dig into God's Word with you as we experience its transforming power together.

DAY 1: THE FATHER'S GLORIOUS PLAN

Focal Point

Begin today's study by reading Ephesians 1:1-6.

Masterpiece. You are the handiwork of the most magnificent Artist who created you in His image, rescued you from darkness, and placed His Holy Spirit within you as His seal of authenticity. While Michelangelo famously sculpted the statue of David from marble, God carved the mountains of earth out of nothing. While Leonardo da Vinci blended paint to bring the *Mona Lisa*'s smile to canvas, God breathed the universe into existence, painting solar systems of light. Each of these artists is considered masters of their craft, yet each was created by The Artist who breathed life into their bodies, inspiration into their souls, and talent into their beings. God is the Ultimate Artist who fashioned us in His divine image to reflect His glory.

The word *masterpiece* speaks to our core identity. This week we dive into Ephesians and discover riches that will forever change how we view ourselves and our God. Today we behold the heart of our heavenly Father, who devised a plan so magnificent that it required the greatest sacrifice imaginable to rescue us and adopt us into His family.

God, the Father

Scripture reveals God as a Trinity—Father, Son, and Holy Spirit. While the purpose of this study is not to delve into this weighty concept, we will discover this week a glorious truth: each person of the Trinity is intricately involved in our salvation. Today we begin by learning about the role of God our Father, which proves vital to knowing the truth of our redeemed identity as His beloved children.

The Big Picture
Ephesians is easily divided into two distinct halves. Chapters 1–3 focus on our position in Christ as God's masterpiece, and chapters 4–6 center on how we practically live in this world.

All praise to God, the Father of our Lord Jesus Christ, who has blessed us with every spiritual blessing in the heavenly realms because we are united with Christ.

EPHESIANS 1:3 NLT

Let's begin by reading all of Ephesians 1. If you are comfortable marking in your Bible, identify every reference to God the Father with a box or yellow highlighter. Be sure to mark any pronouns (he, his) that refer to God the Father.

Examples:

Verse 2: "Grace to you and peace from God our Father and the Lord Jesus Christ."

Verse 6: "to the praise of his glorious grace."

What truths jumped off the page as you read and marked references to God the Father?

Now let's turn our attention back to our Focal Point, Ephesians 1:1-6. As a reminder, last week we prepped the canvas, establishing the who, what, when, where, and why of Ephesians. Now in verse 3 the focus shifts to the message of this letter.

Read Ephesians 1:3 in the margin. To whom is all praise given?

What was done that deserves such praise?

Where are these spiritual blessings found?

We receive these spiritual blessings because we are _____ with Christ.

To best understand the phrase "spiritual blessings," imagine you are on a television game show, and you've been told you won the grand prize. You wait with breathless anticipation for the host to unveil what awaits you as the winner. This is what Paul does for us now. He excitedly reveals the riches and blessings the Father has bestowed upon us because we are *in Christ*.

Read Ephesians 1:4 in the margin. When did God the Father choose you to be His own?

If we are "in Christ," how are we seen in the eyes of God the Father?

Stop and ponder this truth with me. Before God spoke the universe into existence, He saw you. He loved you. He chose you. If you're anything like me, you may have struggled with feelings of rejection your whole life, but let me assure you of one thing—you were never rejected by God!

Relish in the fact that if you are "in Christ," you are without fault in God's eyes. What freedom! What confidence! What boldness we have to approach our heavenly Father knowing that He isn't angry at our sin or frustrated with our failures. Truly, in Jesus you are holy and without fault!

How does the truth that being in Christ means God sees you as "holy and without fault" strike your heart today?

Now read Ephesians 1:5 in the margin. What did God the Father decide "before the creation of the world" to do for you?

Adoption is dear to my heart. My own mother was an orphan. She and her siblings were literally left on the streets as babies. If not for

Even before he made the world, God loved us and chose us in Christ to be holy and without fault in his eyes.
EPHESIANS 1:4 NLT

God decided in advance to adopt us into his own family by bringing us to himself through Jesus Christ. This is what he wanted to do, and it gave him great pleasure.
EPHESIANS 1:5 NLT

> See how great a love the Father has bestowed on us, that we would be called children of God.
>
> *1 JOHN 3:1 NASB*

the kindness of strangers, my mother's story would have been vastly different. Through adoption, my mom was given a home, a family, and a new name. The same is true for you and me—when we put our faith in Christ, we are given a new home, a new identity, and a new destiny. Now, because of Jesus, we are children of God.

Verse 5 also declares that adopting you into His family gave God "great pleasure." What gives you great pleasure?

First, I love to dance with my husband. I also love riding horses. Much of my life is filled with deadlines and demands, but when I'm on horseback, I feel free. While both of those things are pleasurable, nothing gives me more joy than seeing my daughter explore new things. Although motherhood is filled with challenges, being a mom is one of life's sweetest pleasures.

As we think about pleasure, please don't miss this: God took "great pleasure" in choosing and adopting *you* as His child. I emphasize this point because some of us feel that God loves the world but merely tolerates us. Many of us struggle to believe that God truly loves us.

Read 1 John 3:1 in the margin. How do you respond to the declaration that God delights in loving you?

It is crucial we believe that we are children of God in whom He delights. This belief forms the foundation of our identity. We cannot live as God's masterpiece unless we first believe we are chosen and loved by Him. Even as a redeemed woman of God, I struggled for years with severe insecurity. It wasn't until I came to believe the truths about my identity found in Ephesians that my life began to change. Can you relate in any way?

How has your life been marked or marred by insecurity?

Comprehending the depths of God's love transformed everything about me, and I pray it does the same for you. Being adopted into God's family is not just a big theological concept; this truth proves to be heart-healing medicine. Embracing the fact that we are beloved changes how we see God and ourselves. First John 4:18 states, "Perfect love casts out fear." When you believe you are perfectly loved by God, it drives out every fear that torments the soul. Fears of rejection, abandonment, failure, and death are banished by resting in the love of the Father. Instead of a life of chronic insecurity, you can know in the deepest places of your heart that you are both accepted and cherished. Nothing and no one can change that fact. You need not fear failure, rejection, or not being good enough, thin enough, or pretty enough. Why? Because the ultimate authority has already declared that in Jesus, you are enough!

But why does it prove so difficult for some of us to receive this truth? While we can read the words on the page and even say them aloud, there is a distinct difference between reading and receiving. I have found that a common source of this unbelief lies in our unhealed father wounds.

Addressing Our Father Wounds

I once made an absolutely wretched mistake as a Bible teacher. I was speaking at a women's conference and prepared a message about God's lavish love for us. My misstep occurred in the opening seconds of my talk. I began with an emotional scene from the movie *Hope Floats*. It's an oldie but a goodie. Sandra Bullock plays Birdie, a woman whose husband abandoned her for another woman. Her daughter, Bernice, is left in the position that millions of girls face every day—living in a divorced home without a father. If you've seen this movie, then you know the gut-wrenching scene I'm about to describe. Little Bernice stands outside as her daddy packs his bags and drives away. Bernice chases down her father's car, sobbing and screaming, "Daddy, Daddy!" It's one of the most heartbreaking moments captured on film. I've seen it countless times, and not once have I watched without tears flowing down my cheeks.

My intention was good; I wanted to expose the pain earthly fathers can inflict while at the same time reveal how we have a

We cannot live as God's masterpiece unless we first believe we are chosen and loved by Him.

loving heavenly Father who longs to heal every broken place in our souls. What I didn't calculate into my planning was the immense pain many in the room who had experienced this type of abandonment personally would feel. I deeply regret I didn't walk with more sensitivity into this moment. Many couldn't even hear my words of comfort because they were overcome with grief. I vastly underestimated how deeply their earthly fathers had wounded them.

I learned from this experience one of the most important truths of my ministry: many women are deeply wounded by their fathers. This tender reality is one that our study of Ephesians will address and, I pray, will guide each of us to the heart of a loving heavenly Father who longs to envelop us in His love. But I know a painful reality: many women can't relate to God as a loving Father because of wounds experienced by their earthly fathers. Perhaps that includes you.

What was your relationship like with your father as a child, and how has this relationship (or lack thereof) shaped the woman you've become?

How might you have projected the image of your earthly father onto God, your heavenly Father?

Women across the globe suffer from insecurity and feelings of unworthiness. Often this insecurity can be traced back to damage done to their hearts—sometimes, though certainly not always, by absent or abusive fathers. Because we live in a broken world, even wonderful fathers can fail us from time to time, not loving us in the ways that we need. Some of these wounds were unintentional, but, sadly, some were not. Yet regardless of the nature of our relationship with our earthly fathers, all of us need a revelation of God as our loving heavenly Father.

Today I have a wonderful relationship with my dad. I call him regularly for advice and prayers. But that was not always the case. As a little girl, I suffered from a deep wound of abandonment. When someone outside of my family abused me, I misinterpreted the events of my childhood in such a way that I believed my dad didn't love me. Although my dad didn't know about the abuse, my young heart simply believed I was unloved because I wasn't protected. As a result, I projected an image of an absent and uncaring earthly father onto God, my heavenly Father.

One of the first things the Lord did when He began the work of transformation in my life was to heal my heart and help me understand His love as my heavenly Father. Why? Because we can't know who we are as His masterpiece until we first know who we are as His beloved child. Neil Anderson writes,

> The most important belief that we possess is a true knowledge of who God is. The second most important belief is who we are as children of God. . . . If we do not see ourselves as God sees us, then to that degree we suffer from a wrong identity and a poor image of who we really are. It is not what we do that determines who we are. It is who we are that determines what we do.[1]

Wherever you are, stop and say to yourself, "I am chosen and loved by God." Now, take a moment to close your eyes and invite God, your heavenly Father, to affirm these words to you personally.

I pray you will allow this truth to penetrate the places in your heart where you feel unwanted or unloved. No matter your experience with your earthly father—whether he was awesome or absent, adoring or abusive—you have a good Father who chose you to be His own before the foundation of the world. He adopted you into His family so that He could display His glorious grace through you—His masterpiece!

Prayer

In the space below, connect with God using your own words:

No matter your experience with your earthly father . . . you have a good Father who chose you to be His own before the foundation of the world.

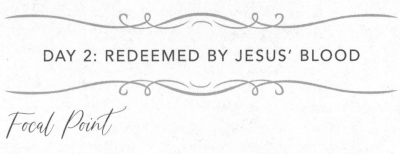

DAY 2: REDEEMED BY JESUS' BLOOD

Focal Point

Begin today's study by reading Ephesians 1:7-10.

I don't know of any words penned by a mere mortal that summarize the heart of Ephesians better than "O For a Thousand Tongues to Sing" by Charles Wesley. (If you aren't familiar with it, then please go to YouTube and listen to it!) I'll never forget the moment I first read each stanza of this most beloved hymn. Sitting by the ocean at a church retreat, I was overwhelmed with the majesty of these lyrics and, more so, how they expressed every emotion I felt toward Jesus for rescuing me from my sin and graciously giving me new life . . . all for the glory of His great name. These words in particular pierced my heart:

> He breaks the power of canceled sin,
> he sets the prisoner free;
> his blood can make the foulest clean;
> his blood availed for me.

Today we will dive deeper into Ephesians 1 and see firsthand why Charles Wesley and others have longed for "a thousand tongues to sing" praises to God for the triumphs of His grace. We will turn our eyes upon Jesus and behold His blood that can make the foulest clean.

Read today's Focal Point, Ephesians 1:7-10. Note how are we redeemed: "through his _____" (v. 7)

If the thought of blood makes you a little squeamish, fear not! Today's lesson will help us understand why Charles Wesley penned such rapturous praise about the blood of Christ, and I pray each of us walks away with a deeper awe and devotion to the One who paid the ultimate price to set us free!

Redemption Through His Blood

One of my favorite Bible teachers, J. M. Boice, writes, "Redemption is central to Christianity. More than that, it is probably the single most beloved term in all the Christian's vocabulary."[2] I wholeheartedly agree with this sentiment! No one is too far gone for grace. Jesus can take the biggest mess and make a masterpiece!

The word for "redemption" in the Greek is *apolutrosis*, which is also translated as "ransom."[3] This language implies captivity, bondage, or slavery. Scripture describes sin as something that controls us and holds us captive. Here's the thing: our culture doesn't like to talk about sin. We dismiss it, deny it, or downright ignore it. The problem with this approach is that we can't truly experience freedom if we don't understand that we are in bondage to something we can't escape on our own. We are desperate for a Redeemer to set us free.

Jesus Himself described His work as our Redeemer.

Read John 8:34-36 in the margin. How did Jesus describe the condition of those who sin?

Is there anything in your life you've felt powerless against? A sinful habit you couldn't break or a temptation you couldn't resist? Name it below, or describe how it makes you feel.

What did Jesus say the Son of God is able to do?

Jesus taught that sin isn't just something we have (like a cold virus); sin is something that has us. It is something that holds us in captivity, refusing to let us go. We don't have control over it; it has control over us. The picture is a slave controlled by a master. Sin holds us

> "Very truly I tell you, everyone who sins is a slave to sin. Now a slave has no permanent place in the family, but a son belongs to it forever. So if the Son sets you free, you will be free indeed."
> *JOHN 8:34-36 NIV*

For all have sinned
and fall short
of the glory of
God, and all are
justified freely by
his grace through
the redemption
that came by
Christ Jesus. God
presented Christ
as a sacrifice
of atonement,
through the
shedding of his
blood—to be
received by faith.

ROMANS 3:23-25 NIV

The Big Picture

For more in-depth study, read the full Passover account in Exodus 12:1-27.

captive and refuses to let us go unless a ransom is paid, which is precisely what God did to solve our problem.

Read Romans 3:23-25 in the margin. What did God present His son as?

A sacrifice of _____ through the shedding of his _____.

Jesus clearly understood His mission (Mark 10:45). He came to be the ransom that would set humanity free from the bondage of sin. But how would He accomplish this great redemption? How was the ransom for our souls paid? The apostle Peter answers this important question for us.

You were not redeemed with perishable things like silver or gold from your futile way of life inherited from your forefathers, but with precious blood, as of a lamb unblemished and spotless, the blood of Christ.

1 PETER 1:19 NASB

In 1 Peter 1:18-19, how are we redeemed?

"With the precious _____ of Christ, a _____ unblemished and spotless."

Let's explore the meaning of this verse and how Jesus' blood was the atonement for our sin, redeeming us for the glory of God.

Behold the Lamb

Scarlet threads of prophecy weave throughout Scripture to reveal a glorious tapestry of redemption. One such prophetic symbol is the sacrificial lamb. I believe it is virtually impossible to understand the New Testament and the ministry of Jesus Christ unless we understand the significance of the sacrificial system of the Old Testament, in which lambs were sacrificed in the Temple as an act of worship to God and the means of atonement for sin.

The lamb played another significant role during the Feast of Passover, which celebrated when God delivered His people from slavery in Egypt with ten miraculous plagues against their enemy, Pharaoh. The last and final plague was the death of the firstborn.

Israel had been in slavery in Egypt for around four hundred years (see Genesis 15:13; Exodus 12:40-41; Acts 7:6; and Galatians 3:16-17). They were oppressed, beaten, and subjected to cruel masters. They cried out to the Lord for deliverance. God delivered them by the leadership of Moses through a series of plagues against Pharaoh and the Egyptians (Exodus 6–11). God gave Moses specific instructions for His people to save them from this final plague. Each family was to kill a spotless lamb and put its blood on the doorposts of their home. Next, the entire family was to remain inside, under the covering of the blood. The death angel would "pass over" and see the blood, and that home would be saved. Those under the covering of the blood would be granted life, instead of death. To be delivered from death required the blood of a substitute.

Now, let's open the New Testament and see how Jesus was the fulfillment of this prophetic symbol by serving as our substitute sacrifice. Read John 1:29 in the margin.

What title is given to Jesus in this text?

What did Jesus come to do?

Jesus, Our Passover Lamb

Jesus understood that He came from heaven to earth to give His life as a sacrifice of atonement. During His earthly ministry, He was pushed by followers and skeptics alike to prove that He was the Messiah. However, time and again Jesus responded with the simple statement, "My time has not yet come" (John 2:4; 7:6). Time . . . what time? You see, Christ knew that He came to die as the final sacrifice for sin and that, as the perfect Lamb of God, He must die on Passover. Therefore, as we read through the Gospels, we see

The next day John saw Jesus coming toward him and said, "Look, the Lamb of God, who takes away the sin of the world!"
JOHN 1:29 NIV

The Big Picture
Atonement: *The word atonement means to "cover over." The sacrificial lamb served as a substitute. Instead of a man or woman dying for his or her sins, God provided the lamb to take the place of that person, and the blood of the lamb paid the penalty for their sin—covering over their sin.*

When Jesus had finished teaching, he told his disciples, "You know that two days from now will be Passover. That is when the Son of Man will be handed over to his enemies and nailed to a cross."
MATTHEW 26:1-2 CEV

The Big Picture
Read the prophetic words found in Isaiah 53.

a dramatic shift. As the Feast of Passover draws near, Jesus finally declares that His time has come!

Read Matthew 26:1-2 in the margin. What event was coming in two days, and what did Jesus say would happen to Him on this day?

The night before Jesus was crucified, He gathered to eat the Passover meal with His disciples. For centuries, Israelite families came together to remember the Passover event and the lamb's blood that "covered them" and gave them life. Through a symbolic meal, they praised God for His mighty deliverance. In that moment, Jesus took the bread and wine and said, "This is my body. . . . This is my blood . . ., which is poured out for many for the forgiveness of sins" (Matthew 26:26, 28 NIV). With these words, he declared himself the fulfillment of the Passover symbol.

Just as significant as His words, the specific details of His crucifixion leave us without a doubt that He is our ultimate Deliver, our Passover Lamb. After celebrating the Passover meal, Jesus led His disciples to the garden of Gethsemane, where the Roman soldiers would arrest Him and take Him to the Jewish leaders, who would see that He was sentenced to death.

Friday dawned and Jesus was led to a hill outside the city walls of Jerusalem. Jewish tradition tells us that at the third hour (9:00 a.m.) Israel's High Priest tied the Passover lamb to the altar in the Temple for sacrifice.[4] At that exact moment, Jesus was nailed to the cross (Mark 15:22-25). For six brutal hours both the Passover lamb and Jesus drew closer and closer to tasting death. At noon the sky turned dark, and it seemed like darkness won. While Jesus was tortured, mocked, and forsaken, He endured the full penalty for sin (Romans 3:21-31). Finally, at the ninth hour (3:00 p.m.), the High Priest ascended the altar in the temple and sacrificed the Passover lamb at the exact moment that Jesus uttered his final words and died (Mark 15:33-37).

Blood spilled out. The lambs were slain. As John records in his Gospel, Christ's words thundered out over the city of Jerusalem before he died, "It is finished!" (John 19:30). Jesus breathed His last.

He lived a sinless, perfect life, proving that He alone was qualified to be the ultimate sacrifice. Then He died the death we should have died so that death and judgment would "pass over" us. Precious friend, this is the glorious truth Ephesians refers to when it says "we have redemption through His blood" (Ephesians 1:7 NIV).

Now that we understand the significance of these words, open your Bible and read today's Focal Point, Ephesians 1:7-10. What does this truth tell you about God's heart for you?

How does understanding the significance of the sacrificial lamb help you appreciate the forgiveness and freedom Jesus lavished upon you?

How does seeing the price Jesus paid to redeem you change how you see yourself?

I've often heard that something is worth what someone is willing to pay for it. So many women struggle with feelings of insecurity and doubt their worth, and as a result their lives reflect this line of thinking. Living as God's masterpiece begins with knowing and believing the depth of His love for you. Just think: God paid the ultimate price to redeem you! Your value was settled in heaven before the foundation of the world. Jesus said you were worth dying for!

Prayer

In the space below, connect with God using your own words:

> *Your value was settled in heaven before the foundation of the world. Jesus said you were worth dying for!*

DAY 3: SPIRITUAL BLESSINGS IN CHRIST

Focal Point

Begin today's study by reading Ephesians 1:7-12.

Years ago, when I was a young, broke, and adventurous college student, I traveled to California for spring break with a few friends. We did all the usual touristy activities like seeing the Hollywood Walk of Fame, rollerblading down Venice Beach, and shopping on Rodeo Drive. Our big goal for the trip was to be on the television game show *The Price Is Right*. As the show began, I was beyond shocked when the host called my name saying, "Marian Jordan . . . come on down . . . you are the first contestant on *The Price Is Right*."

Stunned, I walked down the aisle with eyes bugged out, dazed by the bright lights and fanfare of the game show. Before I knew what was happening, I found myself bidding on an item and stepping on stage with Bob Barker, the longtime host of the show. The next few minutes whizzed by as I nervously played games, gave the wheel a spin, and won prize after prize. To my utter shock, I walked away from the CBS studios with cash, trips, and furniture! As a young, broke college student, this was the biggest thing that had ever happened in my life.

Initially, I couldn't really process all that had happened. But once I stepped into our taxi to head to the airport, the reality hit me—I JUST WON ON *THE PRICE IS RIGHT*! I could not contain my excitement. I gushed to anyone who would listen. First, our taxi driver heard the whole tale; then upon arriving at the airport, I actually ran into a famous celebrity, Robert Redford, and divulged to him the entire story from start to finish! (His bodyguard asked me to step back more than once.) Then once we boarded our flight home, I began to describe the entire show to anyone on the flight who would listen. Once back at our university, my sorority threw a big party to watch the episode when it aired on television.

As I remember the glee I felt after winning *The Price Is Right*, I'm reminded of how the apostle Paul opens his letter to the church in Ephesus. Paul absolutely gushes with praise to God for the glorious work of redemption. He can't stop expressing gratitude for the incredible gifts that are showered upon us when we are in Christ. Paul describes these gifts as "spiritual blessings," and throughout chapter 1 he enumerates what these blessings are.

Once again read all of Ephesians, chapters 1–6. I promise you that there is great treasure awaiting you as you discover your spiritual blessings "in Christ." If you are comfortable marking in your Bible, underline every reference to your position "in Christ." Look for phrases such as these:

<u>in him</u>   <u>in Christ</u>   <u>with Christ</u>

<u>in the beloved</u>   <u>united with Christ</u>

Inheritance

As we read through Ephesians, we discover our spiritual blessings are found "in Christ." Jesus is our access to the immeasurable riches of God. Renowned Bible teacher Warren Wiersbe makes an interesting observation about the city of Ephesus that sheds light on how the church there would have understood the meaning of our spiritual blessings "in Christ."

> The fact that Paul is writing about wealth would be significant to his readers, because Ephesus was considered the bank of Asia. One of the seven wonders of the world, the great temple of Diana, was in Ephesus, and was not only a center for idolatrous worship, but also a depository for wealth. Some of the greatest art treasures of the ancient world were housed in this magnificent building.[5]

Since the city of Ephesus was recognized as the banking capital of the Roman world, it would have been easy for the recipients of this letter to comprehend the meaning of "in Christ." Just as material

In Jesus Christ we are righteous before a Holy God, free from any shred of condemnation, and empowered by Christ in us to live an abundant life beyond our wildest imaginations.

wealth is held *in* a financial institution, so the wealth of God is found "*in Christ.*" All of the spiritual blessings that belong to us as God's children are found "in Him" and "with Him" in the heavenly places.

Now that you've marked where these key phrases are found in Ephesians, take a few minutes to note what is true of us if we are "in Christ." Read the verses below and record what you learn about yourself:

Ephesians 1:4   I am . . .

Ephesians 1:5-6   I am . . .

Ephesians 1:7   I have . . .

Ephesians 1:11   I have . . .

Ephesians 1:13   I am . . .

Ephesians 2:5   I am . . .

Ephesians 2:6   I am . . .

Ephesians 2:10   I am . . .

No wonder the apostle Paul gushes as he marvels at all God the Father has accomplished for us in Christ. Our spiritual inheritance is rich indeed! As a Christian, we put our hope in Jesus, for it is "in Him" that we find forgiveness, acceptance, love, freedom, and victory. As we continue through this study, we will learn more about our position in Christ—how, as a child of God, we live in this world although our true spiritual home and identity are in the heavenly realms with Christ.

Friend, in Jesus Christ we are righteous before a Holy God, free from any shred of condemnation, and empowered by Christ in us to live an abundant life beyond our wildest imaginations. Ephesians summarizes all that is ours "in Christ" by saying that "in Him . . . we have obtained an inheritance" (1:10-11 KJV). Now, what does Scripture mean by *inheritance*?

When I was a little girl, I loved the movie *Annie*. In this beloved musical, a curly red-headed orphan with freckles and a spunky spirit named Annie is trapped and abused by a wicked guardian, but in the most stunning act of redemption, she is adopted by a wealthy businessman who becomes her father. Little Annie is transported from poverty to riches and becomes the heir to a great fortune. Her inheritance is beyond imagination. This story illustrates the greatest story of all, the gospel. When we put our hope "in Christ," we are set free from a cruel master and gloriously adopted into God's family. Now as His sons and daughters, we are heirs of the kingdom of God. Paul explains this idea in Galatians 4:4-7 in the margin.

According to this passage, why did God send his Son? (v. 5)

What has changed in us because of God's work of redemption? (v. 7)

You are an heir of the kingdom of God. This is a profound truth that, when rightly understood, can radically change a person's entire outlook on life. Like Annie, you've been set free and brought into the family of God, where your Abba Father calls you His beloved and loves to lavish you with every spiritual blessing. Friend, this is your inheritance!

Biblically speaking, *inheritance* refers to "the complete experience of the salvation that God promises to his people but which they have yet to receive in full. This experience culminates in their redemption upon Jesus' return."[6] Inheritance has a present tense reality and holds a future tense promise. Presently, we are set free from the domain of darkness, and our future hope is full restoration with God in heaven. As the apostle Peter explains:

[3]Blessed be the God and Father of our Lord Jesus Christ! According to his great mercy, he has caused us to be born again to a living hope through the resurrection of Jesus Christ from the dead, [4]to an inheritance that is imperishable, undefiled, and unfading, kept in heaven for you, [5]who by God's power are being guarded through faith for a salvation ready to be revealed in the last time.
1 PETER 1:3-5

[4]But when the fullness of the time came, God sent forth His Son, born of a woman, born under the Law, [5]so that He might redeem those who were under the Law, that we might receive adoption as sons. [6]Because you are sons, God has sent forth the Spirit of His Son into our hearts, crying, "Abba! Father!" [7]Therefore you are no longer a slave, but a son; and if a son, then an heir through God.
GALATIANS 4:4-7 NASB

What three words are used to describe our inheritance?

Where is this inheritance kept for you?

Our spiritual inheritance points to the eternal future we have with Christ. How does the truth and hope of this future give you confidence and joy in the midst of hard circumstances?

Dear friend, I pray your heart has been moved today by all the riches that are yours *in Christ*. Ephesians unfolds for us the treasures found in Jesus. Far greater than winning a silly game show, we are recipients of an eternal inheritance that can never spoil or fade away. Over the course of this study, we will discover more and more of what our inheritance is and how we can appropriate these riches into our daily lives. Spend a few minutes processing with the Lord all that you learned today and giving Him praise for your position in Christ as His beloved child.

Prayer

In the space below, connect with God using your own words:

DAY 4: THE SPIRIT-SEALED INHERITANCE

Focal Point

Begin today's study by reading Ephesians 1:13-14.

I'll never forget the night Justin asked me to be his wife. We were preparing to meet friends on New Year's Eve when he pulled off the sweetest surprise engagement. To say I was shocked is an understatement! When Justin hit his knee and revealed a beautiful diamond ring, all I could do was shriek with joy and exclaim, *"Are you proposing?"* After he assured me that yes, he was indeed asking me to marry him, I finally allowed myself to feel the elation that only a giddy bride-to-be can feel. He slipped the ring on my finger and I stared in wonder at the shimmering symbol of our commitment.

I share our engagement story because today's portion of Ephesians emphasizes the Holy Spirit's role in our redemption. Like an engagement ring that is given as a token of devotion and a promise of future commitment, so, too, the Holy Spirit is given to God's children as the promise of our eternal inheritance in Christ.

This week in our study of Ephesians we're discovering how each person of the Trinity is actively involved in our salvation. First, we beheld the lavish love of God the Father and His plan to adopt us into His family. Next, we learned that this great work required the sacrificial death of Jesus, the Son of God, who paid the ransom price for our sins. Today we turn our attention to the Holy Spirit.

Let's begin by examining the text and understanding who the Holy Spirit is and what He accomplishes in the work of redemption.

Read Ephesians 1:13 in the margin and complete the following:

This verse states that we who "heard the Good News . . . and trusted Christ" were _____ as "belonging to Christ by the _____ _____."

> And because of what Christ did, all you others too, who heard the Good News about how to be saved, and trusted Christ, were marked as belonging to Christ by the Holy Spirit, who long ago had been promised to all of us Christians.
>
> *EPHESIANS 1:13 TLB*

³⁷On the last and greatest day of the festival, Jesus stood and said in a loud voice, "Let anyone who is thirsty come to me and drink. ³⁸Whoever believes in me, as Scripture has said, rivers of living water will flow from within them." ³⁹By this he meant the Spirit, whom those who believed in him were later to receive. Up to that time the Spirit had not been given, since Jesus had not yet been glorified.

JOHN 7:37-39 NIV

The phrase "marked as belonging to Christ" means there is a distinct characteristic or defining quality that sets apart a genuine follower of Christ from the world. It is the evidence that someone belongs to Jesus. In the Book of Acts, after Jesus' resurrection, the early disciples were under intense pressure by the religious leaders (the same ones who sentenced Jesus to death) to stop telling people about Jesus. No matter how much these religious leaders tried to silence those early disciples, they would not stop proclaiming what they had witnessed. The writer of Acts makes a special note about Peter and John, saying that the religious leaders were astonished by their boldness and recognized that they had been with Jesus (Acts 4:13). This is striking considering that when Jesus was sentenced to death, both of these men ran in fear. What had changed in the few short weeks since Jesus' crucifixion that had radically altered these men? First, both Peter and John were eyewitnesses to the Resurrection. They knew for a fact that Jesus defeated death and conquered the grave. As eyewitnesses they were transformed from fearful followers to faithful leaders. But there was something else that set these men apart. Although they were uneducated and untrained men, they could powerfully proclaim the Scriptures and testify to Jesus as the long-awaited Messiah in ways that their opponents could not refute. Why? Because they now had the Holy Spirit empowering them!

Forty days after Jesus' ascension (Acts 1:6-9), the disciples were in Jerusalem for the Feast of Pentecost (Acts 2) when they were gathered together and the Holy Spirit was poured out upon them. Now those first disciples were filled with power from God! This is precisely why Paul says in our focal passage that we are marked as belonging to Christ by the Holy Spirit.

Ephesians 1:13 declares that whoever trusts in Jesus as Savior receives the Holy Spirit. There isn't a special club or group of Christians who receive the Spirit; actually, the evidence that someone is a Christian is the fact that the Holy Spirit is in his or her life. Jesus states something similar in the Gospel of John:

Read John 7:37-39. What did Jesus say would happen to whoever believes in Him? (v. 38)

To whom does "rivers of living water" refer? (v. 39)

Just as my wedding ring indicates to the world that I'm married to Justin Ellis, so, too, the Holy Spirit marks a believer as belonging to Christ. We will discover more in upcoming days about the power and fruit of the Spirit in a believer's life, but our primary purpose today is to learn how the Holy Spirit of God seals our salvation. As it says in 2 Corinthians 1:21-22, "Now it is God who establishes both us and you in Christ. He anointed us, *placed His seal on us,* and put His Spirit in our hearts as a pledge of what is to come" (Berean Study Bible [BSB], emphasis added).

A seal in the ancient Roman world served to authenticate a document and to guarantee the contents were genuine. A king would sign an official decree, pour wax upon the document, and then press a signet ring bearing his image into the hot wax, forming a seal. This seal authenticated the decree and proved to the world that the document was legitimate. In the same way, the Spirit of God proves to the world that we are children of God because we bear His image. The Holy Spirit fills us with God's love (Romans 5:5), confirms that we are His children (Romans 8:15-16), and helps us to become like Christ (Galatians 5:22-23). The Holy Spirit is both the outward mark and inner assurance that one is a child of God.

In today's Focal Point passage, we see that the Holy Spirit was promised to us by God long ago (v. 13). In this statement, the apostle Paul refers to both the Old Testament prophecies and Jesus' promises in the New Testament concerning the gift of the Holy Spirit. Let's dig into God's word and discover more about these promises.

Read the following verses and note what you learn about the Holy Spirit:

Isaiah 44:1-5

Joel 2:28

> The Holy Spirit marks a believer as belonging to Christ.

The Holy Spirit is God's "guarantee" to us that He will complete the work of redemption.

Ezekiel 36:26-27

John 16:7-15 (Note: In this passage Jesus describes the Holy Spirit as the "Helper," "Comforter," or "Advocate," depending upon your translation.)

Acts 1:1-9

Based upon all of these Scriptures, summarize in your own words the purpose of the Holy Spirit:

After I trusted Christ as my Savior, I immediately began to see evidence of the Holy Spirit that confirmed I was genuinely a child of God. Before this I did not have conviction of sin, but now I felt the weight of my sin and how it displeased God. I experienced new desires to please God whereas formerly I only wanted to please myself. I sensed a new hunger to know Jesus more and to grow in my relationship with Him. I also felt a new power over temptation that I had not been able to resist in the past. Also, without adequate words to explain what was happening inside of me, I would often tell people that I felt "alive" for the first time in my life. This new life, power, conviction, and hunger for truth was evidence of the Spirit working in my life. As a result, His presence gave me confidence and assurance of my salvation—which is precisely what a seal is meant to do! Remember, in the Roman era, seals were used to authenticate and guarantee ownership. I knew without a doubt that I was a child of God because of His Spirit working in my life. I knew I belonged to Jesus!

What about you? In what ways have you seen evidence of the Holy Spirit working in your life?

Now that we know more about the promise of the Holy Spirit, let's look at His role in our redemption.

Read Ephesians 1:14 in the margin, and circle the action of God that is repeated.

What does the Holy Spirit guarantee us?

The Holy Spirit is God's "guarantee" to us that He will complete the work of redemption. Writing to the Corinthians Paul said, "God . . . has given us the Spirit as a deposit, guaranteeing what is to come" (2 Corinthians 5:5 NIV). This again reminds us of an engagement ring, which is a very powerful symbol of an existing love and a future marriage. As one Bible scholar notes, "Thus the Holy Spirit symbolizes the love of God and promises that we shall someday share in His glorious home."[7]

Friend, have you ever struggled with assurance of your salvation? If so, write about it briefly:

How does the idea that God guarantees your redemption speak to your heart?

Dear friend, I pray you comprehend the depth of God's commitment to you. He is so earnest in His pursuit of you that He guarantees your full redemption and eternal security with His very own Spirit. He deposits the Holy Spirit into your life the moment you trust in Jesus as your Savior. Remember, Jesus said when we believe we receive. As we grow in our relationship with God, it is the ministry of the Holy Spirit within us that gives us boldness, confidence, and assurance that we are, indeed, children of God!

His presence within us is God's guarantee that he really will give us all that he promised; and the Spirit's seal upon us means that God has already purchased us and that he guarantees to bring us to himself. This is just one more reason for us to praise our glorious God.
EPHESIANS 1:14 TLB

The Big Picture

In Greek, the word for "guarantee" is also translated as "earnest." Like earnest money that guarantees a home buyer will fulfill all of the requirements to fully purchase the home, the Holy Spirit is the "guarantee" of our inheritance. God is so sincere in His plan to redeem us that He has deposited His very own Spirit into our lives as the sign that He will keep His promise.

Take a few minutes to process and pray through what you've learned today about the Holy Spirit, asking God for continued evidence that you belong to Jesus!

Prayer

In the space below, connect with God using your own words:

DAY 5: RESURRECTION POWER

Focal Point

Begin today's study by reading Ephesians 1:15-23.

Today I'm writing from the airport in Istanbul, Turkey, which, coincidentally, is just hours from the ancient city of Ephesus. I'm traveling home from Israel, where I've been teaching the Bible in the Holy Land. We toured the places where Jesus ministered, performed miracles, taught about the kingdom of God, and was crucified for our redemption. Yesterday we ended our tour with a visit to the Garden Tomb in Jerusalem where Jesus was buried, and, more important, was resurrected. As we gathered in the beautiful garden, we marveled at the empty grave and the fact that Jesus conquered sin and death for us. To conclude our time together we sang one of my favorite old hymns, "Victory in Jesus."

Here's the thing about victory in Jesus: It's one thing to sing about it and a far different thing to experience it. Friend, victory is our inheritance, and it was accomplished for us when Christ the King rose from the dead and ascended to heaven. From His position of victory we can stand victorious. While this is the bedrock truth of Christianity, far too few who claim the name of Christ experience the triumph He gives us. Far too many of us are defeated by

> addictions,
> insecurity,
> anxiety,
> shame,
> perfectionism, or
> bitterness.

Do you feel like you are walking in victory or defeat? Why?

Many years after I experienced the redeeming grace we've been studying this week, I still lived defeated by bitterness, shame, and the unhealed wounds from my childhood. But, praise God, I've tasted victory because of the truths found in Ephesians! I can sing "Victory in Jesus" from authentic experience. I'm far from perfect, but day by day and year by year I've learned to stand firm in Christ and take hold of the power Jesus offers.

The Bible emphatically declares that those of us who are in Christ are more than conquerors (Romans 8:31-39). Although we battle against temptations, darkness, and oppression, the ultimate reality for us is that we are positioned with Christ Jesus in His triumph: "But thanks be to God! He gives us the victory through our Lord Jesus Christ" (1 Corinthians 15:57 NIV).

Remember, it was Jesus who said, "You will know the truth, and the truth will set you free"(John 8:32 NIV). I firmly believe the key to living the victorious Christian life is found in *first* comprehending who we are as children of God and *then* applying this truth to our daily lives. As we dive into God's Word today we will discover how His resurrection power equips us to live in victory.

Reread today's Focal Point, Ephesians 1:15-23, which is the longest prayer in the New Testament. Then answer the following questions:

What two things has Paul heard about the Ephesians? (v. 15)

"your _____ in the Lord Jesus and your love _____ toward all the saints"

Paul has heard that these believers are standing firm in their faith in the midst of trials and that they are exhibiting love for one another. Faith and love are the external evidence of an inner transformation, evidence that genuine salvation has occurred. Why? *Faith* is an expression of our trust in God (a vertical relationship), whereas *love* is evidence of our right relationship with others (a horizontal relationship).

As a result of what he has heard, what does Paul do? (v. 16)

To whom does Paul address his prayers? (v. 17)

"the God of our Lord Jesus Christ, the Father of _____ "

Notice how Paul addresses his prayer to God the Father. He does not pray to an unapproachable, distant deity but to One he knows as Abba, which is the Hebrew name for Father (Romans 8:15). Paul models for us prayer that approaches God as a beloved child would approach a compassionate Father.

We too can experience this intimate relationship with God because His Son, Jesus, has made the way possible (John 1:12). Friend, our prayers reflect how we see God.

What image of God comes to mind when you pray? Is He near or far? Is He caring or callous? Is He inviting or demanding?

It took me years to realize I was hesitant to approach God as my Father because I believed lies about His heart. (As we discussed on Day 1 of this week, our image of God as Father is often marred by experiences with our earthly fathers.) I struggled to believe God loved me and wanted me in His presence. As my understanding of God grew through the study of His Word, I comprehended more of His goodness and love. This revelation in turn transformed how I approached Him. Now I pray with boldness, believing my God is for me and not against me. I stand on the truth of Scripture, which gives me assurance of my relationship with Him as His beloved daughter.

According to verse 17, what does Paul pray that the Father would give to them?

"The Spirit of _____"

Paul does not pray that we would know more facts about God but that we would truly *know* Him. I could learn countless facts about a famous celebrity and not actually know that person at all. There is a vast difference between the two. Paul's prayer is for us to experience an intimate relationship with God.

It's often said that Christianity is not a religion but a relationship. God wants us to walk with Him, to hear His voice, to experience His nearness, and to draw near to Him in love. The relationship that Jesus invites us into is one in which we respond to His lavish grace with devotion and dependence. Therefore, Paul prays for us to experience a deeper revelation of God that propels us to even deeper knowledge of Him.

Review Ephesians 1:15-19 again and note the three things Paul precisely prays for us. (Note: This wording is based on the English Standard Version; other translations will vary.)

". . . having the eyes of your hearts enlightened, that you may know . . ."

"the _____ to which he has called you" (v. 18)

> Now this is eternal life: that they know you, the only true God, and Jesus Christ, whom you have sent.
> JOHN 17:3 NIV

69

"the riches of his glorious _____ in the saints" (v. 18)

"the immeasurable greatness of his _____ toward us who believe" (v. 19)

This type of knowledge is not of the intellect but of the experience. It is one thing to know from a postcard that Florida beaches have white sand and crystal blue water, and it's a far different thing to curl your toes in the sand and stare out at the endless ocean as the sun rises upon the horizon. Paul prays we would know Jesus' power from genuine *experience*.

Now read the conclusion of this prayer in verses 19-23 and answer the following questions:

Who is Jesus' power for? (v. 19)

When was this incomparably great power demonstrated? (v. 20)

Where is Christ Jesus seated today? (vv. 20-21)

What is under the feet of Jesus? (v. 22)

The incomparably great power of God that is available for us today was demonstrated when Jesus rose from the grave. This miracle is a proven historical fact. As Billy Graham wrote, "There is more evidence that Jesus rose from the dead than there is that

Julius Caesar ever lived or that Alexander the Great died at the age of thirty-three."[8] Over five hundred eyewitnesses beheld the resurrected Christ, but most important, those witnesses demonstrated a new power as a result of their relationship with Him. Evangelist and Bible teacher Watchman Nee wrote, "Our old history ends with the Cross; our new history begins with the resurrection."[9] Because Jesus reigns victorious, we too can live victoriously. One commentary notes:

> The power Christians have is not intrinsic power, something they have in themselves, but a power that comes from God, defined by the resurrection of Jesus and his exaltation as Lord over every other power, both now and in the future. Because no other power can rival him, and because in him the fullness of God lives, Christians do not have to look elsewhere to find what they need for life. What they need is in Christ. This power, however, is not power in the abstract, it is *relational power*—power that is known because of being bound to the one in whom power resides.[10]

How do we access this power? God's Word reveals the key to victory is simply to acknowledge our weakness and confess our dependence upon Jesus. This may sound obvious, but the key to victory is recognizing that we desperately need Jesus' power! This requires humility, but it also demands faith. Humility confesses, "God, I need you." Faith believes, "God, only you can provide the strength to do what is impossible in my own power." This relational power is accessed through relying upon Christ and trusting Him moment by moment to supply our needs. Friend, even the great apostle Paul acknowledged his desperation for God's power!

Read 2 Corinthians 12:9 in the margin and answer the following: In what is God's power made perfect?

In what did Paul boast?

The key to victory is simply to acknowledge our weakness and confess our dependence upon Jesus.

But he said to me, "My grace is sufficient for you, for my power is made perfect in weakness." Therefore I will boast all the more gladly about my weaknesses, so that Christ's power may rest on me.
2 CORINTHIANS 12:9 NIV

> ¹⁵For we do not have a high priest who is unable to sympathize with our weaknesses, but one who in every respect has been tempted as we are, yet without sin. ¹⁶Let us then with confidence draw near to the throne of grace, that we may receive mercy and find grace to help in time of need.
>
> *HEBREWS 4:15-16*

What was the result of his boast?

Now it is your turn. Where do you feel weak and in need of God's power today?

The Bible makes one thing crystal clear: when it comes to spiritual power and blessings, we have not because we ask not (see Matthew 7:7). Jesus, who is seated at the right hand of God the Father, lives to make intercession for us. This means He is acting on our behalf and in tune to our needs and prayers.

Now read Hebrews 4:15-16 in the margin. What is Jesus, our high priest, able to do?

What will we find at the throne of grace?

Relish in the fact that your weakness is the place where you can experience God's great strength. What "weakness" do you want to see God's power evident in today?

Whatever you wrote above, go ahead and ask God for it! When we come to Jesus, He is ready to pour out His power to help us in our time of need. In God's economy, victory comes from dependence upon the One who holds the victory. Acknowledging our desperate need and asking Jesus for His power is the key to winning the war. Friend, let's bring our brokenness and weaknesses to the throne of grace where we meet the God of mercy who empowers us for victory! As you conclude your time in God's Word today, open your heart to Him and confess the areas where you feel weak and want to experience His resurrection power!

Prayer

In the space below, connect with God using your own words:

In God's economy, victory comes from dependence upon the One who holds the victory.

SESSION 3: VIDEO VIEWER GUIDE

Ephesians 1:15-23 – Paul's prayer for us to have revelation knowledge of who we are in Christ

Ephesians 2:1-10 – Who we are

1. The Bible says if you are in Christ, you are a _____ .

Ephesians 1:1 – We are saints

Saint – a person who has been chosen and set apart by God, who is justified by faith in Jesus Christ, and who is sanctified by the Spirit of God, who offers their lives in sacrificial service to God and pursues holiness in both motive and practice.

2. We are _____ children of God.

3. You are God's _____ .

Who are you going to give the right to name you?

WEEK 3: GOD'S MASTERPIECE

Overview

In Ephesians 1, Paul looked at our redemption from God's point of view, showing how He blessed us in Christ with a spiritual inheritance. Now, as we proceed into chapters 2 and 3, we will learn about the gift of salvation from the perspective of the individual who is redeemed. We will discover who we were before God rescued us, what God did for us in delivering us from the domain of darkness, and who we are as the result of that divine deliverance. Each day this week you'll discover an element of your new identity in Christ. Get ready to discover *who you are* as God's masterpiece!

DAY 1: YOU ARE SAVED BY GRACE

Focal Point

Begin today's study by reading Ephesians 2:1-7.

C. S. Lewis's beloved children's novel *The Lion, the Witch, and the Wardrobe* tells the story of four children who enter a magical wardrobe and find themselves involved in a fight between forces of good and evil in the land of Narnia. In this allegory of the Christian life, Narnia is ruled by an evil White Witch, who symbolizes Satan. She has subjected Narnia to a perpetual winter, enslaving its inhabitants and turning many of them to statues of stone. The arrival of the children sparks a revolt among the Narnians, who believe a prophecy that when the four children appear in Narnia, the Lion Aslan, who symbolizes Jesus Christ, will return to overthrow the forces of evil.

One of the four children, mischievous Edmund, is deceived by the White Witch and as a result becomes her captive. The Witch informs Aslan that she will not relinquish her claim on Edmund, who by law must die for his act of betrayal. In a sheer display of mercy, Aslan offers himself to the Witch in Edmund's place, a vivid picture of Jesus' sacrificial death for undeserving humanity.

The White Witch binds Aslan to an altar and kills him. In the dark of night, the Witch believes she has won. She has no idea about the drastic turn of events about to occur. The children spend a hopeless night weeping beside Aslan's body. However, with the coming of dawn, Aslan miraculously comes back to life. Now Aslan, the resurrected King of Narnia, triumphantly leads the forces of good in a decisive victory over the Witch and her hellish followers. The entire narrative illustrates the death and resurrection of Jesus Christ.

Aslan's first act after his resurrection is to reverse the curse the Witch placed upon Narnia. Winter becomes spring. Then Aslan marches to the Witch's castle, where she held the citizens of Narnia enslaved as stone statues. Aslan breathes on the stone statues and they come back come to life!

C. S. Lewis masterfully illustrates Jesus' victory over the domain of darkness. Just as Aslan breathes upon the stone statues and they supernaturally awaken to life, Ephesians declares that this same miracle occurs in each redeemed soul that is brought from spiritual death to life by the power of God.

Last week in our study of Ephesians, we learned of our spiritual *possessions* in Christ; this week we will learn of our spiritual *position* in Christ. Today we will discover how we are taken out of the great graveyard of sin and placed into the throne room of glory.

Read today's Focal Point, Ephesians 2:1-7. As you do, imagine the power and grace of Jesus that brings us from spiritual death to life. How does your heart respond to these verses?

If this were an extreme makeover show, we would call these verses our "before and after pictures." First we see the bleakest terms possible to describe the human condition apart from God's saving grace (our before picture), and then we learn of our new status in Christ (our after picture).

What is the desperate state of humanity in verse 1?

Warren Wiersbe explains the desperation of the human condition by saying this:

> The unbeliever is not sick; he is dead! He does not need resuscitation; he needs resurrection. All lost sinners are dead, and the only difference between one sinner and another is the state of decay. The lost derelict on skid row may be more decayed outwardly than the unsaved society leader, but both are dead in sin—and one corpse cannot be more dead than another! This means

The Lord moves toward us in kindness, mercy, and grace out of a sheer act of love.

that our world is one vast graveyard, filled with people who are dead while they live.[1]

Look back at verse 1. What two words describe what we are "dead in" before faith in Christ?

_____ and _____

At this point, a few definitions will help us better understand our condition apart from God's grace.

The English word *trespasses* essentially means to detour from a designated path. Imagine you are driving down the road and your car's navigation system informs you to take a right, but you willingly turn left instead. Although this is the wrong direction and you will not arrive at your desired destination, you proceed heedlessly. This is the essence of trespasses—a willfulness to do wrong that results in detouring from righteousness.

The word *sin* is from the Greek *hamartia*, which originally had the idea of missing the mark, as when hunting with a bow and arrow. Later it came to mean missing or falling short of any standard. *Hamartia* in the Bible means to miss God's mark as an archer misses the "bull's eye" and, ultimately, to miss the true purpose and end of our lives, which is God Himself.[2]

Together, these two terms, *trespasses* and *sins*, depict the condition of the human heart. We've turned away from God, chosen our own way, and fallen short of His glorious standard. As Romans 3:23 states, "For all have sinned and fall short of the glory of God."

Now back to today's Focal Point. According to verses 2-3, who and what did we follow in our state of sin?

Comprehending our before picture helps us appreciate God's grace all the more. First we were "following the course of this world" and second we were "following the prince of the power of the air" (Ephesians 2:2). Before we are redeemed, we are captive to this world system that is ruled by the enemy that opposes God and His kingdom.

Read Colossians 1:12-13 in the margin. What are we rescued from?

Why did God rescue us? Why did He set us free from the dominion of darkness? Let's be clear about one thing—He was not obligated to redeem us. The Lord moves toward us in kindness, mercy, and grace out of a sheer act of love. This is what makes grace so amazing! The apostle Paul sums up the miraculous movement of a Holy God toward undeserving sinners with two stunning words: *but God!*

Read verses 4-7 of our Focal Point and complete the following. (Note: This wording is based on the English Standard Version; other translations will vary.)

In what is God rich? (v. 4)

What did God do as a result of His love for us?
"made us _____" (v. 5)

Finally, and most important, how are we made alive?
"by _____ you have been _____" (v. 5)

God has "raised us up with him [Jesus] and _____ us with him in _____ in Christ Jesus." (v. 6)

Let's try to wrap our hearts and minds around this magnificent truth. While we were spiritually dead in our sins, God still loved us. He showed us mercy. He knew we couldn't free ourselves from the powers that held us, so in the greatest act of love the world has ever known, He gave himself as our ransom. *But God!* I think those might be my favorite two words in the entire Bible. "But God" changes everything!

This portion of Ephesians moves from past tense to present tense with ease. Now we behold our glorious position in Christ because of grace. Grasping the reality of your current position as

> [12] Giving joyful thanks to the Father, who has qualified you to share in the inheritance of his holy people in the kingdom of light. [13] For he has rescued us from the dominion of darkness and brought us into the kingdom of the Son he loves.
>
> *COLOSSIANS 1:12-13 NIV*

The Big Picture

"For Christianity begins not with a big DO, but with a big DONE. Thus Ephesians opens with the statement that God has "blessed us with every spiritual blessing in the heavenly places in Christ" (1:3) and we are invited at the very outset to sit down and enjoy what God has done for us; not to set out to try and attain it for ourselves."[3]
WATCHMAN NEE

a child of God is literally game-changing. Let's focus our hearts on one of the most important truths taught in Ephesians: if you are a believer in Christ, you are seated with Him in glory!

Ephesians can be summed up in three simple words: *sit, walk, stand.* First we are "seated with Christ" in His victory (chapters 1–2). Next we learn to "walk" in this world as God's masterpieces (chapters 3–5). Finally, we learn to "stand" against the spiritual forces that oppose us (chapter 6). From beginning to end, the Christian life is about relying on what Jesus Christ accomplished for us on the cross and then appropriating this truth into our daily lives.

These spiritual realities prove a little difficult to comprehend, but once we do, they are life-changing. What does it mean to be "seated with Christ"? Watchman Nee explains:

> When we walk or stand we bear on our legs all the weight of our own body, but when we sit down our entire weight rests upon the chair or couch on which we sit. We grow weary when we walk or stand, but we feel rested when we have sat down for a while. In walking or standing we expend a great deal of energy, but when we are seated we relax at once, because the strain no longer falls upon our muscles and nerves but upon something outside of ourselves. So also in the spiritual realm, to sit down is simply to rest our whole weight— our load, ourselves, our future, everything—upon the Lord. We let him bear the responsibility and cease to carry it ourselves.[4]

After carefully reading the quotation above, how would you explain what it means to be "seated with Christ"?

How does being "seated with Christ" illustrate the gift of grace?

In light of what we've studied today, read Jesus' words from Matthew 11 in the margin. What does Jesus offer the weary?

Friend, God's Word declares boldly that we are *saved by grace*. This truth is so fundamental to Christian theology that it proves the bedrock of all we believe. Grace is a gift and it must be received. Our only response is to receive the gift of grace and rest in Jesus, which is what our focal word *seated* implies. One who is seated is not working but resting.

Spend a few minutes today thanking Jesus with a sincere and humble heart for outpouring His grace upon your life. Imagine yourself taking a seat next to Him, and let out a deep sigh as you lean upon Him and rest your weary soul upon the One who saved it.

Prayer

In the space below, connect with God using your own words:

28"Come to me, all you who are weary and burdened, and I will give you rest. 29Take my yoke upon you and learn from me, for I am gentle and humble in heart, and you will find rest for your souls. 30For my yoke is easy and my burden is light."
MATTHEW 11:28-30 NIV

DAY 2: YOU ARE HIS MASTERPIECE

Focal Point

Begin today's study by reading Ephesians 2:8-10.

The *Mona Lisa* is considered the masterpiece of all masterpieces. She is the most celebrated, examined, and valuable painting in the

As God's masterpiece, our lives point to the Master Artist who calls us His own.

world—estimated to be worth $800 million today. Each year millions crowd the Louvre in Paris where the painting hangs, waiting for their turn to snap a photograph of the renowned work of art. She currently resides behind bulletproof glass as a result of repeated attacks—including stones, acid, and even a coffee mug!

The *Mona Lisa* was painted by the Italian artist Leonardo da Vinci. He likely worked on it intermittently over several years, and it is considered unfinished by some art historians. For centuries the portrait was secluded in French palaces, including Napoleon's bedroom, until placed in the Louvre Museum at the turn of the nineteenth century.

It wasn't until the *Mona Lisa* was stolen in the summer of 1911 that she captured worldwide fame. Newspapers spread the story of the crime and photos of her smile across the globe. When the painting finally returned to the Louvre two years later, the world cheered. Historians believe it was the theft of the *Mona Lisa* that made this painting a household name. Today over six million people visit the Louvre each year to behold her mysterious smile.[5] And I'm happy to report that I've been one of them.

When I was a college student, my sister and I traveled to Paris. We had only a few days in the City of Lights, so we tried our best to visit the highlights.

Eiffel Tower (check).

Champs-Élysées (check).

Arc de Triomphe (check).

Notre Dame (check).

After consuming every French tart this side of the Seine, we visited the Louvre, which boasts some of the world's greatest masterpieces, and none more famous than the *Mona Lisa*. It was easy to find her; simply follow the crowds. Huddled with the masses, we peered around fellow tourists pressed close to the bulletproof glass for one glimpse of the enigmatic smile.

What makes this painting so special? Leonardo utilized a painting technique called sfumato (which means "smoke" in Italian). In this tedious process, paint is applied in thin layers, allowed to dry, and then painted over again (a few hundred times). It's an ancient technique that very few people mastered. One other thing that makes the *Mona Lisa* so special is the fact that her eyes were drawn in a way that they follow you when you move. This difficult optical illusion is achieved by a unique painting technique.[6] With the precision, skill, and mastery involved in this painting, it is no wonder it is considered the masterpiece of all masterpieces, revealing the sheer genius of Leonardo da Vinci.

Just as the *Mona Lisa* displays da Vinci's brilliance, this is the mind-boggling reality that Ephesians drives home: we, the redeemed, exhibit God's glory to the world. This is the message the apostle Paul wants us to grasp in this epistle. We are God's masterpiece through which His love, mercy, wisdom, and power are manifested! As God's masterpiece, our lives point to the Master Artist who calls us His own. He transforms us by His grace so that our lives showcase His goodness. I hope this concept forever changes how you see yourself—how your life is meant to magnify the greatness of our God.

I love how today's Focal Point expresses this idea so beautifully. Let's back up and read it in context of what comes before it.

Read Ephesians 2:1-10. In light of what we've discussed about the Mona Lisa, *how do you see your life differently after reading these verses?*

The Big Picture

"Before we can learn the sufficiency of God's grace, we must learn the insufficiency of ourselves. . . . Just as grace shines more brilliantly against the dark background of our sin, so it also shines more brilliantly against the background of our human weakness."[7]
JERRY BRIDGES

If the Letter to the Ephesians were a symphony, then verses 8-10, today's Focal Point, would be the crescendo of this magnificent score. The word *crescendo* means a gradual increase in intensity that reaches the loudest point in a piece of music. Imagine cymbals trilling, drums beating, and horns blasting as the conductor leads the orchestra to play with all their might the notes that will leave hearts pounding. Leading up to this crescendo, in verses 1-7 the apostle Paul steadily and progressively increases in passion as he explains the brilliance of God's plan to redeem us from the clutches of sin and death. In breathless wonder, Paul culminates his thoughts with a summary of the grace of God that saves us and the fact that we, the redeemed, are the masterpiece of the Lord God Almighty.

> [8]God saved you by his grace when you believed. And you can't take credit for this; it is a gift from God. [9]Salvation is not a reward for the good things we have done, so none of us can boast about it. [10]For we are God's masterpiece. He has created us anew in Christ Jesus, so we can do the good things he planned for us long ago.
>
> EPHESIANS 2:8-10 NLT

According to verse 8 in the margin, when did God save you?

Finish this sentence: You can't take _____ for this; it is a _____ from God.

Think again about the *Mona Lisa*. The painting is praised because of the skill of the artist. It's not like the canvas or the paints did anything on their own. Without da Vinci's masterful use of light and shadow, there would be nothing to behold. The same is true of us. We owe everything to God's grace. All praise is due to the one who redeemed us. Therefore, Paul repeatedly expresses that God's grace is something we "can't take credit for" or "boast about." Why? Because it is a work of God.

From what you've learned so far about God's mercy and grace, why would boasting be out of the question?

In what ways do we as human beings try to earn God's favor or work our way into His family?

What is something you've been tempted to "boast in" or to believe it makes you more loved by God? (Be honest with yourself.)

Thus far, Ephesians has made it clear that the only way into God's family is through the door marked "grace." By faith we enter and receive the gift of salvation. We can't earn His love or merit His favor, because Christ alone makes the way possible through His sacrifice for our sin. Therefore, it is not about our good deeds, religious practices, or human effort; it is 100 percent about Jesus! As a result, all glory goes to God, and none of us has grounds to boast.

Now that we've well established we are saved by grace through faith in Jesus, let's turn our attention again to the crescendo of Paul's teaching.

According to verse 10, who are you?

Rick Renner notes the significance of the Greek word for masterpiece. He writes,

> This comes from the Greek word *poiema*. It carries the idea of something that is *artfully created*. The Greek word for a poet . . . comes from this same word. . . . The word *poiema* tells you that when you became a child of God God put forth His most powerful and creative effort to make you new. This work emphatically declares that once God was finished making you new, you became a *masterpiece, skillfully and artfully created in Christ Jesus*. There's nothing *cheap* about you at all! *God's creative, artistic, intelligent genius went into your making.*[8]

Look again at verse 10. What does it say is the purpose for which God declared you to be His masterpiece?

Here is the beautiful twist. Though we aren't saved *by* our good works, we are saved *for* good works. As new creations in Christ, our lives display the power, love, and grace of God for the world to see. We live in response to the grace we've received by aligning our lives with His truth, doing the works He created us to do, and being His hands and feet in a broken world. Through our transformed lives we showcase to a watching world that God can take a mess and create a masterpiece.

We respond to God's love with love for our neighbor. We respond to God's mercy with mercy for others. We reflect the glory of God to the world by showcasing His transforming power in our lives. These are the "good things he planned for us long ago" (Ephesians 2:10b NLT). Once we comprehend the depths of God's love, mercy, and grace, our relationship with Him transforms from

*Though we aren't saved **by** our good works, we are saved **for** good works.*

¹⁷Now the Lord is the Spirit, and where the Spirit of the Lord is, there is freedom. ¹⁸And we all, who with unveiled faces contemplate the Lord's glory, are being transformed into his image with ever-increasing glory, which comes from the Lord, who is the Spirit.

2 CORINTHIANS
3:17-18 NIV

duty to delight. As John, the beloved disciple, writes, "We love, because He first loved us" (1 John 4:19 NASB).

Reflection time. Is your relationship with God marked by duty or delight? Do you feel yourself striving to earn His favor or responding to His lavish grace?

God's Workmanship

One of the world's greatest sculptors was Michelangelo. From his chisel came forth the statue *David*. As an artist, he chipped away at a piece of marble until the final product revealed his glorious intention. This is also is the idea presented in Scripture when you and I are declared God's masterpiece. From the moment of our salvation we are His masterpiece, but the fullness of this truth is revealed in our lives over time as God transforms our character to be more like Jesus Christ. By the work of the Holy Spirit, we are being transformed by God into something so magnificent that it showcases His redemptive power and love (see 2 Corinthians 3:17-18). This process is called sanctification, where we become more and more like Jesus in our daily lives and are set apart to do the works He redeemed us to do. All of us who know Christ are in this process.

Think about your own sanctification journey. How are you different today than you were before Christ? How is God transforming you to be more like Jesus?

Tonight my husband and I met with several other couples who compose our Life Group. These men and women are our Jesus community. Each week we study God's Word together and someone shares how God is working in his or her life. We call these testimonies, but I like to think of them as Masterpiece stories. As we share how the Lord is shaping and molding our lives, it is like taking a front-row seat to behold the Master at work. Each story is unique, but the unmistakable hand of the Artist is displayed in each person. God's brilliant artistry weaves together strands of darkness and light to create a tapestry of beauty.

Before Jesus, my life was riddled with sin and darkness—I was a liar, thief, glutton, and addict. I was prone to rebellion, anger, jealousy, and pride. On that first day of my new life in Christ, I wasn't much different; but over time the new person God was creating began to emerge. Over the next few months, I noticed changes in my behavior, and so did others. These changes didn't occur because I was trying hard to obey rules or act religious; these changes occurred because my heart was different. Now I wanted to glorify God instead of living for myself. I no longer wanted to indulge in the dark lifestyle of sin that once held me captive.

Truth replaced lies. Obedience replaced rebellion. Love replaced selfishness.

I'm not saying I was instantly perfect or sinless; I'm just saying a new person existed inside of me, and she was beginning to shine. As these changes occurred, I knew it was a work of God—not something of which I could boast. Sometimes I felt like I was watching myself react in such a different manner that I would marvel, "That's Jesus, not Marian!" People who knew me before and after Jesus would also marvel at the changes, and I would sincerely proclaim, "Amazing grace how sweet the sound that saved a wretch like me."

Over time, God burdened my heart for the ministry that He had created for me to do. First, I started teaching Bible study in my local church, then women's conferences began asking me to speak, and then God opened doors for me to write books. Day by day, I stepped into the "good works" that He had prepared for me to do. If you had asked me before I knew Jesus if I would be writing this Bible study today, I would have laughed in your face. I was terrified of public speaking and didn't know the first thing about Scripture. But God knew what He had gifted and called me to do long before I ever did. We will discuss spiritual gifts more in coming days, but I'll be honest: I didn't know what my gifts were until I just started doing something.

Dare to dream with God. What do you imagine God created you to do for His glory?

Remember, as God's masterpiece your good works don't earn you God's love; they are the evidence of His artistic handiwork, and His creative power is working in you. You are a reflection of the handiwork of the Divine Artist to a watching world!

Prayer

In the space below, connect with God using your own words:

DAY 3: YOU ARE THE TEMPLE OF THE HOLY SPIRIT

Focal Point

Begin today's study by reading Ephesians 2:11-21.

Recently I stood on the Temple Mount in Jerusalem and taught about God's plan to redeem us through the sacrificial death of His Son. It was on that very spot where countless lambs were placed upon the altar and spilled their blood to atone for sin—a foreshadowing of Jesus' death on the cross.

The Temple holds great significance in the Bible as the place where God's people worshiped Him. Understanding the sacrificial system and the importance of the Temple helps us comprehend much of Scripture. Both the Old and New Testaments are filled with references to the Temple; and as we turn to Ephesians, there is an underlying assumption that the readers of this letter are familiar with the worship, sacrifices, and historical significance of the Temple.

As I concluded my message that day on the Temple Mount in

Jerusalem, our local tour guide began to describe the eagerness of the Jewish people to rebuild their Temple that was destroyed thousands of years ago and how this rebuilding would fulfill biblical prophecy. While I'm a big fan of watching biblical prophecy unfold, I could sense confusion and questions amid my group: *Will we worship God as they did in the Old Testament? Will God require the sacrifice of animals?* I watched their eyes widen in wonder as they considered the ramification of such an event. At that point I stepped in to remind them of one vital truth: *As Christians, we don't require a physical temple to worship God, because the Bible says that we, His people, are now the temple in which He dwells.*

This marvelous truth is the focal point of today's lesson. As Christ's followers, *we* are now the temple of God's Holy Spirit. While many of us have heard the expression that we are the temple, this truth would have been radical news to the ears of the Ephesians. For this reason, the apostle Paul requires us to wade through some deep theology before coming to the shore of this incredible reality. Before arriving at our destination, we first must learn of the work God did to reconcile two distinct groups of people into one.

Before we dig into the rich theology found in our Focal Point, take a few minutes to review the passage. If you are comfortable marking in your Bible, circle the words you, our, *and* us.

What are your initial observations about this passage?

What do you discover about these two groups of people?

Paul's aim in Ephesians is to summarize the gospel message and explain how it remakes us as God's masterpiece. In order to achieve this goal, he must address some issues that were affecting the church of his day—primarily the division between Jews and Gentiles. Let's quickly explore these two groups and some related key terms.

As we studied in Week 1, the original recipient of this letter was the church in Ephesus, which comprised both Gentile and Jewish followers of Jesus, otherwise known in today's text as "the circumcised" and "the uncircumcised." A Gentile was anyone who was not Jewish. Since Ephesus was a Roman city, the church was filled with Gentiles who grew up in a vastly different culture with different religious practices than the Jewish people. (I just have to point out that the beauty of the gospel is that it reaches across cultures, languages, and races, bringing all who hope in Christ Jesus into one family with one heartbeat.) One practice that was not shared between the two groups was circumcision.

Circumcision is the ritual act of removing a male child's foreskin eight days after birth (see Genesis 17:12). As part of the covenant that God established with Abraham, every male living with Abraham, "both he who is born in your house and he who is bought with your money" (Genesis 17:13), was to be circumcised.[9] Circumcision was a physical symbol of God's covenant with Abraham, the father of the Jewish people. Anyone who was not a descendant of Abraham and was not circumcised was called the uncircumcised, or a Gentile.

This covenant with Abraham was a *divine covenant*, which is a binding agreement or promise initiated by God between Himself and one or more other parties. There are two forms of divine covenants: conditional and unconditional. A *conditional covenant* is a covenant with conditions placed on the humans involved. The Gospel Coalition explains,

> Think of it as an "if, then" promise by God. If the person does A, then God will do B. . . . An unconditional covenant is . . . a covenant with no conditions placed on the promises made. There is no "if, then" aspect. God simply promises to do something. Because these divine covenants are initiated by God, they are backed by His character. That is why they are absolutely reliable. Furthermore, they are initiated by God for His glory and our good.[10]

The covenant God made with Abraham, called the Abrahamic Covenant, is an example of an unconditional covenant. God made promises to Abraham that required nothing of Abraham. There are three main features to the Abrahamic Covenant: God's promise of land, God's promise of descendants or a nation, and God's promise of blessings and redemption (see Genesis 12:1-3).

The covenant God made with Moses hundreds of years later, called the Mosaic Covenant, was a conditional covenant that was centered around God giving His divine law to Moses on Mount Sinai (see Exodus 19–34). The Mosaic Covenant differs significantly from the Abrahamic Covenant because the blessings that God promises are directly related to Israel's obedience to the Mosaic Law (Exodus 19:3-7).

Although the Mosaic Covenant was conditional, it served to reconfirm the covenant with Abraham. Here's a brief summary of the five divine promises of the Mosaic covenant:

1. Israel will be God's special possession.
2. Israel will be a kingdom of priests to God.
3. Israel will be a holy nation.
4. God will fight for Israel and overcome all her enemies.
5. God will treat Israel with grace and mercy and forgive her sins.

I share this background material and explain the various covenants because the apostle Paul assumes his readers hold a basic knowledge of these terms when he writes this epistle, and I believe that understanding these covenants is key to understanding much of the Bible.

Reread Ephesians 2:11-12. What was once true of the Gentiles (before Jesus)? List everything you see in these verses.

Fill in the blanks according to verse 13:
"But now in _____ _____
you who once were _____ _____
have been _____ _____ by
the _____ of Christ."

Now carefully read verses 14-17, and circle every instance of the word **peace***. How many times do you see this word in these verses?*

"Let them
construct a
sanctuary for Me,
that I may dwell
among them."
EXODUS 25:8 NASB

What is true of the Gentiles (aka "the uncircumcised") now because of Jesus? List everything you see in verses 18-21.

According to verse 21, what are both the Jews and Gentiles "joined together" to form?

Paul is saying in these verses that the Jews and Gentiles (the circumcised and uncircumcised) were once two distinct people. They were once divided because the Jews were included in God's covenants, given the Law and access to the Temple, while the Gentiles were excluded from these things. The great news Paul is communicating is that now, in Christ, all of that has changed. All who follow Christ are now one people, one body called the church—brought together by Jesus to be the temple where the Spirit of God dwells.

Today *we* are part of the church. You and I are the temple of God! To grasp the absolute wonder of this reality and how it transforms everything about our identity, let's learn more about the Temple.

The Book of Exodus recounts God's deliverance of His people from slavery in Egypt, which foreshadows our deliverance from slavery to sin. After Moses led the Hebrews out of Egypt, they entered the wilderness where God initiated the covenant we've already explored and instructed Moses in the building of the Tabernacle. This tabernacle was the original blueprint for the Temple. Let's take note of God's motive for having the people construct the sanctuary.

Read Exodus 25:8 in the margin. What was God's desire?

Just marvel at this fact: God desires to dwell with us. What was lost in the garden of Eden, He restores. He is the initiator of relationship and has created a way for us to be in His presence. The Old Testament Tabernacle and temple and all of the sacrifices performed there all pointed forward to Jesus Christ who perfectly fulfilled each symbol and sacrifice and who is the ultimate way that we can access the presence of God.

Now turn to 1 Kings 8:1-10. This story recounts King Solomon's construction of the Temple in Jerusalem to worship the Lord. After the construction was completed, the priests brought the ark of the covenant into the Holy of Holies. According to verse 10, what happened once the Temple was completed?

Here is where all the puzzle pieces come together. The cloud that filled the Temple was the presence of God. The Scriptures tell us that when the Lord delivered the Israelites out of slavery in Egypt, He led them out with a cloud by day and a fire by night (Exodus 13:20-22). This cloud is called the "Shekinah Glory of His Presence." Later in Exodus we are told that the Lord spoke to Moses out of the pillar of the cloud (Exodus 33:11). So, when we see the cloud filling the Temple that Solomon built, we know that this cloud is the very presence of God filling the Temple. As we absorb these details, this should cause us to marvel that Ephesians declares we are now the temple of God, the very place where God's spirit dwells.

Look up the following verses and record what you discover:

Ezekiel 36:26-27

1 Corinthians 3:16

1 Corinthians 6:19-20

Ephesians 2:22

Ephesians declares we are now the temple of God, the very place where God's spirit dwells.

Based upon all you've learned today, how would you answer this question: **What are you?**

Given that Scripture declares a Christian is the temple of God's Spirit, where His glory dwells, what implications does this truth hold for your daily life?

Friend, you are not common, ordinary, or insignificant! The glory of God dwells within you. You don't have to go to a physical location in order to meet with Jesus because you can meet with Him wherever you are! He is not only with you; His very Spirit dwells within you!

Prayer

In the space below, connect with God using your own words:

DAY 4: YOU ARE THE CHURCH

Focal Point

Begin today's study by reading Ephesians 3:1-13.

This past weekend I attended a wedding in Charleston, South Carolina. My belly is full from a weekend of eating delicious food like shrimp and grits and biscuits coated with honey butter that was simply "slap yo momma good"! Aside from eating my way through a foodie's paradise, I also toured historical sites and learned that Charleston is known as the Holy City. When I asked a guide why, she replied, "Because there is a church on every corner."

Her comment stuck with me because it reminded me how the world views the church. Many assume it is a building or a location, but this is not a biblical understanding of the word. The word *church* in Scripture is a translation of the Greek word *ekklesia*, which means the "called-out ones."[11] The root meaning of the church is not a building but a people. The word *ekklesia* implies all that we've covered so far in Ephesians. God, who is rich in mercy, has called us out of the darkness and set us free to live in His marvelous light. We are the "called-out ones," and this is the biblical understanding of who and what the church is.

In our study today, we lean into one of the most profound ideas in the Bible and especially in Ephesians: through the church, God displays His glory to the world.

Friend, you and I are the church. The church is not a building; it is not a program; it is a people. While many images spring to mind when people read this word, I hope today's study gives you a greater love and appreciation for the church and your role within her.

Look again at our Focal Point, Ephesians 3:1-13. Read it once more slowly before answering the questions that follow.

What three words begin verse 1?

The words "for this reason" refer to all that Paul had explained in 2:11-22. One commentary explains the significance of these three words by saying:

> Paul had been arrested in Jerusalem and, eventually, had been imprisoned because he took a stand for the equality of Jews and Gentiles as Christians (believers in Christ). The Jewish antagonists saw Paul's teaching as radical and destructive to temple practices. Thus, Paul

was writing here that he had been imprisoned for the sake of Gentiles. The religious leaders in Jerusalem, who had felt scandalized by Jesus' teachings and didn't believe he was the Messiah, pressured the Romans to arrest Paul . . . and [bring] him to trial for treason and for causing rebellion among the Jews. . . . Paul knew that his imprisonment was by God's will—therefore, he called himself **a prisoner of Christ Jesus** . . . (see 1 Corinthians 4:1; Philippians 1:1; 2 Timothy 1:8).[12]

Paul wrote this epistle as a prisoner in Rome. He viewed his imprisonment as a part of God's greater purpose. Can you look back at a challenging season in your own life and see God's greater purpose through it? If so, write about it briefly:

Read today's Focal Point once more and circle the word **mystery.** *How many times does Paul use this word?*

According to verse 6, what is the mystery?

When Paul uses the term "the mystery," he is not referring to something mysterious as you and I would use that word. Ephesians uses this term to describe something hidden that is now revealed. The mystery is not that Gentiles would be saved, for the Old Testament gave evidence of that; rather, it is that believing Jews and Gentiles are joined together in one body, the church!

According to verse 10, what is God's goal for the church?

One source notes the weight of these words by saying,

> In classical Greek the adjective "manifold"
> (*polypoikilos*) referred to the beauty of an embroidered
> pattern or the variety of colors in flowers. . . .
> The "manifold wisdom of God" does not refer to
> redemption as such but rather to the new relationship
> between believing Jews and Gentiles in one body.[13]

Through the church, God displays His glory, wisdom, and divine plan. It is vital for you and me to understand that we are members of God's body and that, as His church, it is through us that He works out His plan for the world.

How does this insight change or challenge your view of the church?

Don't Date the Church

A friend of mine once dated a guy who later—out of the blue—bailed on their relationship. Fun coffee dates and long romantic talks resulted in an awkward silence. After a frank conversation about his distance, she learned that he held a list of the perfect woman in his mind, and she didn't quite measure up. Ouch, right?

Soon we discovered this was a pattern in his life. Countless beautiful, Jesus-loving women failed his perfection test, and thus he remained alone. The issue wasn't with my friend but with his inability to commit. His unrealistic expectations left him always assuming the grass was greener somewhere else. I'm not trying to criticize men. Women can do the very same thing, looking for the perfect guy. What I want to acknowledge is that all of us can, from time to time, do a similar thing with the church.

Sometimes we Christ-followers can act like that guy or girl who is waiting for the perfect someone. We will "date" the church instead of faithfully committing our lives to Christ and His body. We hop from one service to another, taking good teaching from one place and incredible worship from another, without committing

It is when we give of ourselves, truly investing in the lives of others, that we find true life and discover the joy of Jesus.

ourselves to love, give, and serve alongside a community of believers. Many of us approach the church from a consumer mentality instead of a commitment one.

The problem with this consumer mentality is that it flies in the face of the true meaning of the church. Instead of consumers, we are called to be givers. Givers of our time, resources, and gifts. As we've seen, the church is not a building; it is people—a group of people called out of darkness to live as Christ's ambassadors. We go to the buildings, services, and events to worship, serve, and give—not to be served. So often we miss out on the great and glorious work God wants to do in and through us when we don't commit. Interestingly, it is when we give of ourselves, truly investing in the lives of others, that we find true life and discover the joy of Jesus.

Friend, you are the church and *we* are the church. *We* are the body of Christ, and we are meant to be together.

Let's take a few minutes to discover what God's Word teaches us about the church, the body of Christ. Read the following passages and summarize what you learn from each:

Matthew 18:20

Acts 2:42

1 Corinthians 12:12-27

Hebrews 10:24-25

Each of these passages reminds us of the importance of committing to a local body of believers. Hebrews says we "spur each other on" (NIV). As a woman who loves horses, I get this imagery. Spurs are used to encourage a horse to move in the right direction or run faster. As believers, our gathering together keeps us going in the right direction (toward Jesus) and running the race for which He has called us. Let's consider some of the specific benefits of making this commitment.

Why Commit?

1. We are the church.

Listening to a sermon by your favorite Bible teacher does not substitute for the role God has called you to play in this world. Your active involvement in your local church enables you to use your gifts and talents for the glory of God, which we will explore next week. If you have a complaint, maybe God wants to use you to be the solution. Don't be a critic; be the change. Your spiritual gifts matter, and God works through all of us as we get involved.

How is God calling you to get involved (or more involved) in your local church?

2. We need a squad.

The Christian life is meant to be experienced within community. We need one another. I absolutely do not know where I would be today without the family of God. Through my church family the Lord has provided for my needs, showered His love on me, given me strength and encouragement, and lovingly confronted me in my sin. We are better together!

Who is your squad when it comes to the family of God?

3. We are transformed together.

We are transformed more and more into the image of Christ as we engage in relationship with other Christians. All too often people bail out when a conflict arises in a group or when disappointed with a leader instead of following the biblical guidelines of forgiveness and restitution. It is only within a committed body of believers that we are confronted with our junk and the messiness of others, which requires us to mature. If we run away when times get messy, then we miss out on the beautiful maturing that God wants to do in us and others.

Jesus wants to use your life to display His goodness and grace to the world.

Is there anyone within your local church whom you need to forgive, or with whom you need to seek forgiveness and reconciliation?

Today we've discovered the fact that we don't go to church; we are the church. The church is not a building filled with pews and a steeple on top; it is God's plan for transforming the world. This is His plan A, and there is not a plan B. In Ephesians we behold our new identity in Christ and our purpose as His church.

Jesus wants to use your life to display His goodness and grace to the world. This was God's eternal purpose realized in Christ. He can't do that outside of your involvement and investment in a local community of Christ-followers. Friend, let's go be the church!

Prayer

In the space below, connect with God using your own words:

DAY 5: YOU ARE LAVISHLY LOVED

Focal Point

Begin today's study by reading Ephesians 3:14-21.

Oh, how God loves us! Throughout our study, we've addressed that there is a vast difference between comprehending a biblical truth and apprehending one. For example, I could embrace God's love as a fact but still not experience it personally. To *apprehend* a truth means it becomes part of our core identity and transforms us from the inside out.

I learned the difference between comprehending and apprehending many years ago when speaking at a women's conference. Back then I was riddled with fear that I would disappoint God. Most of my anxiety was rooted in the fact that I didn't truly believe God loved *me*. I could read the words on the page, but the truth never traveled the distance from my head to my heart. Although I loved Jesus passionately, something was missing. I was still a little girl performing to earn her daddy's love—believing the lie I must be perfect to deserve it. You see, I knew of God's love on an intellectual level, but my heart had not apprehended it. The ironic part of this confession is that I was a professional Bible teacher and spent most of my time telling other people about Jesus.

Do you ever feel numb to the fact that God loves you?

I was slated to speak on Saturday morning, so I attended the conference Friday night just like all the other attendees. During worship I observed a group of teenage girls gathered to pray for others. I saw a woman beaming with pride as she watched one of the teenagers. In a split second I realized that was her daughter. Only a mother would watch her child like that. I leaned over and said, "Are you just so proud of her?" Her reply was simple: "You have no idea!" Love was written all over the mother's face.

At that moment, I heard God say, "Marian, *you* have no idea!" The Holy Spirit exposed my unbelief and opened my eyes to apprehend a truth I'd heard a thousand times—*I am a beloved child of God!* In that instant, the worship band began to sing a chorus that says, "Oh, How He loves us!" They repeated this line for about three minutes until I could positively feel the truth as it descended into the depths of my being. (Coincidence? I think not!) As we sang, the weight of God's love sent me to my knees and poured over me. As today's Focal Point says, I experienced the "breadth and length and height and depth" of God's infinite love, "the love . . . that surpasses knowledge" (Ephesians 3:18-19). And friend, I've never been the same since.

Today we turn our attention to Ephesians 3:14-21, which is the bridge between the first and second half of Ephesians. Here we find one of the longest prayers in the New Testament. In this prayer, Paul petitions God on our behalf, praying that we may comprehend the depths of His love and be filled with His strength. This proves the perfect prayer for anyone like me who has ever struggled to believe God loves them—and for all of us as we desire to grow in our experience of God's love. Here we discover how we should pray for ourselves and others to apprehend the lavish love of God.

Today's lesson holds two goals. First, I want this to be more than an intellectual exercise. My prayer is that you experience the depths of God's love for you—whether for the first time or anew today—as you spend time in His Word. My second goal as we walk verse by verse through this passage is that we learn to pray like the apostle Paul, accessing the power and presence of God deep within our spirits.

Learning to Pray with the Apostle Paul

I remember when I was still a sheepish young believer, and I asked a mentor where she learned to pray with such confidence, boldness, and authority. She laughed and said, "From the apostle Paul!" What she meant is that she learned to pray by observing how the great apostle talked to God. Today we will do the same as we allow Paul to model for us *how* to pray. As we do, I pray we experience "the love of Christ that surpasses knowledge [and are] filled with all the fullness of God" (3:19).

Here in Ephesians 3 Paul pauses his teaching and breaks forth in prayer, asking God the Father to strengthen us by His Spirit in our inner being so that we can experience a deeper revelation of His love. This prayer is divided into three parts: *approach God* (verses 14-15), *ask God* (verses 16-19), and *adore God* (verses 20-21). Let's explore each part in detail.

1. Approach God
Look again at today's Focal Point, Ephesians 3:14-21.

What is Paul's posture as he prays?

Paul models for us kneeling before the Lord. We do not need to get legalistic; God hears us wherever we are. We can talk to the Lord while driving, walking, or sitting in our prayer closet. Having said that, our posture does direct our hearts. When I can find a space to kneel, I do so. The physical act of bending my knees reminds my heart that I'm encountering Majesty. The act of kneeling is a small gesture that simply reminds us that we approach a mighty God who upholds the universe with His power and to whom all glory, honor, and praise is due.

To whom does Paul direct His prayer? (v. 4)

Paul prays to God the Father. While Scripture is filled with prayers that are directed to Jesus or the Holy Spirit, the approach that we are taught by Jesus and that we see here modeled by Paul is prayer to the Father. A simple structure to remember is we pray to the Father, in the power of the Spirit, and by the authority of Jesus.

Read Matthew 6:9-13. How did Jesus teach us to approach God?

We approach God as our heavenly Father. It's important to keep in mind that He longs to hear you and is eager for you to come into His presence. Our attitude in prayer is as a child engaging a caring and compassionate Father. As Paul tells us in Romans, "You have not received a spirit that makes you fearful slaves. Instead, you received God's Spirit when he adopted you as his own children. Now we call him, 'Abba, Father'" (Romans 8:15 NLT).

With this in mind, our approach should be a mixture of confidence and humility. On the surface, those attitudes seem to contradict, but in prayer they are essential. We are confident because Jesus has opened wide the door for us to have access to

> This is the confidence we have in approaching God: that if we ask anything according to his will, he hears us.
> *1 JOHN 5:14 NIV*

The Big Picture

There are four requests in Paul's prayer, but they must not be looked on as isolated, individual petitions. These four requests are more like four parts to a telescope. One request leads into the next one, and so on. He prays that the inner man might have spiritual strength, which will, in turn, lead to a deeper experience with Christ. This deeper experience will enable them to "apprehend" (get hold of) God's great love, which will result in their being "filled unto all the fullness of God." So, then, Paul is praying for strength, depth, apprehension, and fullness.[14]

WARREN WIERSBE

the Father (see Hebrews 4:14-16 and 1 John 5:14). This truth is what we've celebrated in Ephesians—we are loved, chosen, and adopted into God's family. We also approach Him humbly because we are mindful that we are in the presence of a holy God, who is worthy of all adoration and worship. We come before Him with humility recognizing our weaknesses but leaning upon His power and strength.

2. Ask God

Reread Ephesians 3:16-19. What four things does Paul request in his prayer?

What does Paul ask that we would be strengthened with? (v. 16)

What does he pray we would be rooted in? (v. 17)

What does he want us to grasp? (vv. 18-19)

Think about your story. Have you ever believed the lie that there was an aspect of your life, personality, or history that was beyond the bounds of God's love? If so, write about it briefly.

God's love is boundless. One commentary beautifully expounds upon this thought: "How big is the love of Christ? how wide? how long? how high? how deep? . . . It is as wide as the outstretched arms of the crucified Savior, embracing Jew and Gentile, rich and poor, male and female . . . reaching out to 'whosoever will.' It reaches low enough to touch the most wretched sinners and high enough to reconcile them to a holy God. . . . How big is his love? As big as the cross."[15]

Nothing fuels faith like the Word of God. Let's spend a few minutes searching the Scriptures to learn more about the love of God. Record what you learn about God's love from each Scripture.

Zephaniah 3:17

John 15:9-17

Romans 5:8

Romans 8:37-39

Why does Paul pray for us to grasp God's love at the deepest level? Because the Christian life is from beginning to end a life of love. First we are invited to experience God's lavish love and then we demonstrate His love to the world. The imagery used in this prayer is of a fountain filling up a vessel to overflowing. Our innermost beings are that vessel that is meant to overflow with the love of Christ.

As we conclude the "Ask" portion of this prayer, review the last part of verse 19. What results when we grasp the love of God "that surpasses knowledge"? What are we filled with?

3. Adore God
Reread Ephesians 3:20-21. What word is repeated in these verses? What is Paul doing here?

Finally, Paul bursts into a doxology, otherwise known as a word of glory to God. Having meditated upon the amazing work of God in redemption and prayed for us to be rooted in Christ's love (Ephesians 1:1–3:19), he ends his prayer with praise to God (3:20-21).

The Big Picture
Today's Focal Point is a parenthetical statement between the first and second halves of Ephesians—the perfect bridge between our belief and our behavior. Chapters 1–3 established the core beliefs of the Christian faith. Chapters 3–6 will focus on how we walk in this world as God's masterpieces.

We can deepen our intimacy with God and experience more of His love by simply asking Him to do this transforming work in us.

To adore God means we express back to Him worship. What fuels this adoration? The doctrinal truths we've learned thus far are what ignites our adoration. As we contemplate all God accomplished in Christ to redeem us, adopt us, and establish us as His masterpiece, heartfelt praise is the only right response.

Now it's your turn. Write your own "doxology" to the Lord. Express your adoration to Him for choosing, loving, adopting, forgiving, and redeeming you for His glory.

Besides exalting the name of our God, Paul's doxology encourages us with the fact that the Lord "is able to do far more abundantly than all that we ask or think, according to the power at work within us" (Ephesians 3:20). Our God is limitless and inexhaustible in power.

Friend, there is no limit to what God can achieve for you, and it is impossible for you to ask Him to do too much. Don't let fear or unbelief hinder your prayers. We are reminded today that our God can do "infinitely more" than we can ask or imagine. One of my favorite expressions I like to use for my own encouragement is "He's got this." I'm a simple woman of faith; my vocabulary is no match for the great apostle Paul's. What this short phrase does for my heart is remind me that there is nothing my God can't provide, accomplish, heal, or restore.

Because you are lavishly loved by God, your prayers are heard by Him! A takeaway for us today is that we can deepen our intimacy with God and experience more of His love by simply asking Him to do this transforming work in us. As we conclude, use the space provided below to approach your heavenly Father with boldness, knowing He longs for you to experience His fullness. He longs for you to ask. Ask your heavenly Father to overflow your life with His endless, boundless love.

Prayer

In the space below, connect with God using your own words:

SESSION 4: VIDEO VIEWER GUIDE

Ephesians 4:1-2 – The "walk" of a Christian (how we live)

Ephesians can be summarized in three words: Sit, Walk, Stand (Watchman Nee)

Ephesians 2:1 – Our former practice

Ephesians 2:10 – Our calling

Walk – equal to one's _____.
.

Old English meaning of worship –
What is worth shipping? What is worthy of my life?
Walking worthy is talking about worship.
Our walk is our daily worship.

A woman who walks worthy is one who will respond to God's amazing grace with _____.

Romans 12:1-2 – An act of worship

A woman who walks worthy _____.
.

Ezekiel 36:26-27 – Transformed from the inside out

Ephesians 4:25-32 – Taking off old behaviors

A woman who walks worthy is going to keep in step with the
_____ _____.

WEEK 4: WALK WORTHY

Overview

This week we find ourselves at the midway point in our study. Ephesians chapters 1 and 2 established who we are in Christ. We are God's masterpiece! Now that we understand our identity, the apostle Paul teaches us how we are to live in response to this revelation. Our calling is to walk worthy of the grace that redeems us and to lay aside our old, sinful nature and put on the new self. I pray the Holy Spirit illuminates these truths to you and speaks directly to your heart as you immerse yourself in God's Word.

DAY 1: CALLED TO WALK WORTHY

Focal Point

Begin today's study by reading Ephesians 4:1-6.

My best friends know a little secret about me—I love all things British. English gardens. Anything penned by the great Jane Austen. The television series *Downton Abbey*. Royal Weddings. Afternoon Tea with scones and clotted cream. Even our family dog is named London!

As a seminary student, I spent a summer studying at Oxford University. This short immersion into British culture only intensified my obsession. Now, back at home in Texas, I get my fix through BBC television and rereading *Pride and Prejudice* for the umpteenth time. Last year I found myself sucked into a miniseries about Queen Elizabeth II called *The Crown*. It's brilliant! The series traces her life from childhood, when her father was the king of England, all the way through the past century and the enthralling details of her reign.

I once heard a popular story told about the queen. It is said that as a young girl, she was racing through the palace and acting extremely childish. As the story goes, her nanny stopped her and asked, "Do you know who you are?" Elizabeth replied, "Why, yes, I'm Elizabeth." Her nanny responded, "No, you are the future queen of England." Her nanny's statement was meant to remind Elizabeth that her conduct and character needed to match her identity. She was not common or ordinary; she was Majesty.

Today we turn a corner in our study of Ephesians and hear the apostle Paul make the same heartfelt appeal to us. We are God's masterpiece, and we are to exhibit this identity in our daily lives. In today's Focal Point we are encouraged to live in such a way that our beliefs and our behavior align—to "walk in a manner worthy of [our] calling" (Ephesians 4:1 NASB).

To see the big picture, let's put our Focal Point in context.

It is not okay for us to claim to be Christians and not reflect our beliefs in our behavior.

Read all of Ephesians 4 and 5. If you are comfortable marking in your Bible, circle every place you see the word walk. *(Note: The NIV translation uses the word* live.)

Share a few insights you gleaned from your initial reading:

In verse 1, Paul says, I "implore you" (NASB). This verb means to urge, to press, to push, or to entreat. This is not a passive request; this calling is from a man eager for us to live worthy of our calling as God's masterpiece.

When was the last time you "pressed" or "implored" someone in a conversation? Why were you so persistent?

In Ephesians 4:1, we are told "to walk in a manner _____ of the _____ to which you have been called."

The word *walk* in this context refers to our manner of living. It speaks to how we conduct our lives. Our call is to walk "worthy." Let's explore what this means.

Walk Worthy

To walk "worthy" means to have equal weight—to be fitting or corresponding to what is expected. As one commentator notes, "It means to have a worth equal to one's position."[1] In Ephesians, we are called to give equal weight to our beliefs and our behavior. It is not okay for us to claim to be Christians and not reflect our beliefs in our behavior. Today, we call this hypocritical behavior, but the Bible calls it living in a manner unworthy of our calling.

In verse 2 of our Focal Point, we discover four characteristics of someone who is walking worthy of their calling. Fill in the blanks with these attributes:

"with all _____ and _____, with _____, showing _____ for one another in love." (Ephesians 4:2 NASB)

Let's dig into each of these characteristics.

Humility is often described as modesty, or the opposite of arrogance. Rick Warren has said, "Humility is not thinking less of yourself, it is thinking of yourself less."[2] Humility reverses the normal drive of the human ego. Instead of putting ourselves first, we put God first, others second, and ourselves last. This call to humility is not a call to self-hatred or a call to ignore self-care but a call to follow the model Jesus gives us to love God and love others.

Summarize what each of the following Scriptures teaches us about humility:

Micah 6:8

Matthew 23:1-12

Philippians 2:3-4

Gentleness (also translated as *meekness*) is a "sensitivity of disposition and kindness of behavior, founded on strength and prompted by love."[3] Gentleness is not weakness but strength that is directed toward others in consideration and grace. It's human power under God's control.

Summarize what each of the following Scriptures teaches us about gentleness or meekness:

Galatians 6:1-2

[1]Therefore I, the prisoner of the Lord, implore you to walk in a manner worthy of the calling with which you have been called, [2]with all humility and gentleness, with patience, showing tolerance for one another in love.

EPHESIANS 4:1-2 NASB

2 Timothy 2:24-25

Titus 3:1-2

Patience can be defined as the capacity or ability to endure delay, trouble, or suffering without becoming upset or angry. A patient woman is not easily agitated and accepts the shortcomings of others with grace. A patient woman does not fly off the handle at every annoyance, but walks with tenderness and understanding toward others.

Summarize what each of the following Scriptures teaches about patience or forbearance:

1 Corinthians 13:4-5

Galatians 5:23-24

Colossians 3:12

Tolerance means to bear with one another in love. Grace is for offenses, and tolerance is for our differences in personality, convictions, and practices. Our secular age claims that tolerance means accepting that each person's own definition of truth is valid—in other words, that there is no absolute truth. This is not the biblical meaning of tolerance. The Bible clearly says there is such a thing as absolute truth, but tolerance, according to Scripture, means we lovingly endure with those with whom we do not agree—whether on matters of belief or conscience.

Summarize what each of the following Scriptures teaches about tolerance or bearing with one another:

Romans 14:1-13

1 Corinthians 13:4-5

1 Peter 3:8-17

Resurrection Power

A few years ago I did a crazy detox cleanse. The purpose was to discover what foods caused allergic reactions in my body. It was dreadful. I had to give up all of my favorite things—coffee, sugar, bread, pasta, cheese . . . did I already mention coffee?

A few days into this ridiculousness, I needed to return something to a local store. With receipt in hand, I waited not-so-patiently in the long return line. When it was finally my turn, my lack of caffeine and intense craving for carbs collided into one fine display of impatience. When the salesperson told me I couldn't return my item, I snapped at her and walked out of the store.

I walked about three steps past the exit when the Holy Spirit convicted me. My attitude was not reflective of Jesus. I acted in pride and arrogance. I wasn't patient; I was rude. The Lord spoke clearly to my heart, "This is *not* walking worthy of your calling." Ouch! I turned around, walked back in, waited again in that long line, and gave that saleswoman a much-needed apology. As Jesus' representative, I had no business treating her or anyone else without kindness and respect.

Each of the four characteristics in today's Focal Point reflects the heart of Jesus. Remember, as God's masterpiece, we are called to "walk" in the power of His Spirit, showing the world that we are new creations in Christ—with or without caffeine! This leads us to an important point: *we can't exhibit any of these attributes in our own strength.* Walking in a manner worthy of our calling isn't something we do in our own power; this character is the fruit of God's Spirit.

Review Ephesians 1:19-21 in the margin. What does verse 20 tell us about the power we have in Christ?

[19]I also pray that you will understand the incredible greatness of God's power for us who believe him. This is the same mighty power [20]that raised Christ from the dead and seated him in the place of honor at God's right hand in the heavenly realms. [21]Now he is far above any ruler or authority or power or leader or anything else—not only in this world but also in the world to come.

EPHESIANS 1:19-21 NLT

113

The Big Picture

"In Essentials Unity, In Non-Essentials Liberty, In All Things Charity."[4]
RUPERTUS MELDENIUS

Remember, we now have the mighty resurrection power of God working in us and through us. Our responsibility is to rely upon His strength and ask the Holy Spirit to exhibit the character of Christ through us. As we rely upon the Holy Spirit, we have the supernatural power of God to exercise patience in the midst of turmoil, humility in the face of offense, and tolerance in enduring one another's differences. God's love fills us and overflows the banks of our hearts to reach others.

Unity. Unity. Unity.

Now, let's turn our attention to *why* Paul implores us to walk worthy. Our calling is to glorify Jesus, the resurrected King who defeated sin and called us from death to life to be His church. Each of these attributes—humility, gentleness, patience, and tolerance—enables us to maintain unity within the church. Because we are the church, comprising different cultures, languages, races, and traditions, it is essential that we strive to maintain unity. The Bible speaks of us as brothers and sisters in Christ; and like any family, there are plenty of things that could divide us. What glorifies God is when we stand as one.

What does Ephesians 4:3 call us to do?

Diligence (or "making every effort," in some translations) implies that we go out of our way to preserve unity. The church in Ephesus was a mixture of Jews and Gentiles from across the Roman Empire. Just imagine the conflicts that would naturally occur when people from such diverse traditions formed one new body. Sure, each person had differing opinions; but in order to maintain harmony, Paul challenged them to focus on the truths they held in common instead of the things that could pull them apart.

Note what Jesus prayed for us moments before His arrest:

[20]*"I am praying not only for these disciples but also for all who will ever believe in me through their message.*

²¹I pray that they will all be one, just as you and I are one—as you are in me, Father, and I am in you. And may they be in us so that the world will believe you sent me."

JOHN 17:20-21 NLT

What, specifically, does Jesus ask for in verse 21?

"that they will all be _____."

Oneness or unity within the church is important to God. We see this reflected in Paul's plea for us to maintain unity. Ephesians 4:4-6 states seven things in which the whole church can agree. These are the basis for unity among all Christians across the globe. The number seven in Scripture is the number of wholeness or completion.

Read Ephesians 4:4-6 in the margin and list all seven of the unifying truths:

One _____   One _____
One _____   One _____
One _____   One _____
One _____

Here Paul lists seven things that can unify all of us as believers: we are members of the same body (Christ's), and we have the same Spirit, hope, Lord, faith, baptism, and God/Father. His repetition of the word *one* emphasizes that we are unified in these primary beliefs. Note also how these seven elements of Christian unity are arranged around each member of the Trinity—the Father, Son, and Holy Spirit. Since Paul has just mentioned the Spirit in Ephesians 4:3, he begins with the Holy Spirit (4:4), moves to Jesus, the Son ("one Lord," 4:5), and ends with "one God and Father" (4:6). While all Christians don't agree on the mode or method of baptism, we do agree on the importance of following the Lord's example of receiving baptism. Keeping the bond of unity means we find the essentials that we do agree upon and hold fast to one another in love.

⁴There is one body and one Spirit—just as you were called to the one hope that belongs to your call—⁵one Lord, one faith, one baptism, ⁶one God and Father of all, who is over all and through all and in all.

EPHESIANS 4:4-6

The church of Jesus Christ may be divided in our eyes; but in the eyes of Jesus, she is one.

As a follower of Jesus, I've experienced the beauty of God's church in all her various forms. I've worshiped with Catholics in Paris; I've prayed with Pentecostals in India; I've studied Scripture with Presbyterians in New England; I've served with Methodists at homeless shelters in Texas. I've shared the gospel alongside Baptists on mission trips. My point is this—the church of Jesus Christ may be divided in our eyes; but in the eyes of Jesus, she is one. What unifies us are these seven core beliefs.

Ephesians teaches us to walk worthy of our calling as God's masterpiece. We do this by allowing the Spirit of God to produce the character of Christ in us. In a world built on ego, selfishness, and pride, we operate in humility, gentleness, patience, and tolerance. In doing so, we glorify our Redeemer and stand unified as His church. And that's a beautiful masterpiece for the world to see!

Prayer

In the space below, connect with God using your own words.

DAY 2: CALLED TO SERVE

Focal Point

Begin today's study by reading Ephesians 4:7-13.

Called. That word carries with it a dual weight of responsibility and identity. First of all, how do I know if I am called? Second, what am I called to do? Finally, what if my calling is not as cool as someone else's? So many questions! So much confusion! And, let's be honest, so much comparison.

There is a strong desire for a sense of calling in our day. We want to live our lives on mission. We want to live for something greater than ourselves. We want to look back and know our time wasn't meaningless. This desire is both good and honorable, but it also proves disappointing if your present situation doesn't seem all that grand or Nobel Prize-worthy. As women who love Jesus, we can often fall in the trap of comparison and think our callings aren't worthy if they aren't on a platform or applauded.

How does the statement "you are called" strike your heart? Does it excite or intimidate you? Do you feel like you are walking in your calling or struggling to know your calling?

I so get it; I've struggled with the pressure of "the call." Let me be clear; I know, without a doubt, I am called. I firmly believe every Christ-follower is. From my very first days of following Jesus (even though I barely knew any of the Bible and was not walking in victory in every area of my life) one thing was sure—I knew my life was not my own anymore. I belonged to Jesus, and my life was His! That was my first sense of calling. The internal drive that says, "Jesus, I am Yours!" Deep within there was the response of surrender to the One who rescued me and gave me life. Long before there were published books, speaking opportunities, or anything resembling full-time ministry, there was a young woman who said, "Jesus, take it all!"

Perhaps you, too, are surrendered. You know your life belongs to Jesus, and you want Him to use your life for something that glorifies His name. Now what? Is your current path the one that Jesus has for you?

In today's Focal Point the apostle Paul declares to those of us who are in Christ that our lives are meant to be lived on mission. This calling echoes Jesus' words in the Great Commission when He told the disciples to "go and make disciples of all nations" (Matthew 28:19 NIV). Jesus made our calling crystal clear: to tell the world about Him and to teach others how to be His disciples. Though each

Each of us is called and equipped with various abilities to further the kingdom of God.

of us will fulfill this calling in different ways using different gifts, we share the same purpose.

As we see in today's Focal Point, Jesus has bestowed spiritual gifts to the church. This means each of us is called and equipped with various abilities to further the kingdom of God.

Look again at Ephesians 4:7-13. What is the purpose of these gifts? (v. 12)

What is the result of each person using her or his spiritual gift? What is accomplished in the church? (v. 13)

The purpose for which God has called and equipped us for service is to build up the body of Christ. As we each discover and use our gifts, we fulfill our God-given mission to make disciples. As we take our place and discover our personal gifting, the result is unity and maturity. In God's plan, we are better together!

What exactly is a spiritual gift? It is a God-given ability distributed to individual Christians by the Holy Spirit. Let's take a quick survey of Scripture to discover more about spiritual gifts.

What gifts are listed in today's Focal Point? (v. 11)

Now read a parallel passage in Romans 12:1-9. What are we called to do in verse 1?

In verse 4, we are told that each of us is part of the body of Christ, but we do not have the same

_____.

Verses 5-9 describe various gifts in the body of Christ. List all seven mentioned here:

Read 1 Corinthians 12:4-11, and write verses 4 and 5 below:

Why is the Spirit given to us? (v. 7)

What gifts are listed in verses 8-10?

It's one thing to read a list of the gifts and to know what your personal gifts are. Often, it proves hard for someone to know his or her gift simply by reading a list. I believe the discovery happens when we begin to serve where we see a need and realize that our passion connects with that need. The big question is this: how do we know where and how God is calling each of us to serve?

To answer that question, let's turn to the Bible and look at Moses. Moses was a man of destiny. His entire life is a miracle in the making. He was rescued as a baby from a death sentence and raised as a prince of Egypt. God set him apart for a great mission. Indeed, he was set apart. Born as a Hebrew slave but raised by a daughter of Pharaoh, Moses was positioned to be the deliverer of God's people from slavery. By examining Moses' life we see how we can discover our calling.

Read Moses' "Burning Bush" encounter in Exodus 3:1-11. What did God call Moses to do? (vv. 7-10)

God always calls us to do something far greater than our ability because that is where we get to see His glory!

We tend to use the "burning bush" as a metaphor for a time when we know God called us to a particular mission. For Moses, it was there at the burning bush that the Lord told him to deliver His people. No big deal; just set free a few million people who were held captive as slaves in Egypt! Friend, God always calls us to do something far greater than our ability because that is where we get to see His glory!

I love Moses' response. His first instinct was to tell God that He picked the wrong guy. He offered up all the reasons why he was not a great candidate. God's response infuses us with hope when we too feel inadequate:

> [10] *"Go. I am sending you to Pharaoh to bring my people the Israelites out of Egypt." [1]Moses answered, "What if they do not believe me or listen to me and say, 'The LORD did not appear to you'?" [2]Then the LORD said to him, "What is that in your hand?"*
>
> EXODUS 3:10; 4:1-2 NIV

What is in your hand? Seems like a random question, right? But it is not. Moses was a shepherd, so in his hand was a shepherd's staff. Just a common, ordinary instrument used to lead sheep. Nothing special. But here we find the amazing thing about the Lord: God uses our "nothing special" in order to do the extraordinary, bringing glory to His great name. He calls us where we are, with abilities we already possess to do "immeasurably more than all we ask or imagine" (Ephesians 3:20 NIV).

The Lord told Moses that he would use that staff in his hand and through it perform miracles, miracles that would deliver His people and show His redeeming love. All God needed was what was in Moses' hand. Moses would now shepherd God's people out of slavery in Egypt.

I have a dear friend who felt burdened by the atrocities of sex trafficking. Her first response was to pray. Then she felt led to recruit other women in our city to join her in prayer. Over time God called her to start a ministry to rescue women who are victims of this horrific injustice. My friend never thought she was a "ministry leader"; she was just a mom who felt burdened to pray for those enduring injustice. What God put "in her hand" was a living room where she could gather other concerned moms for prayer and a passion to see change happen in her city. From that initial step of obedience, God has established a powerful ministry.

What's in Your Hand?

For many years I knew I wanted to serve God, but didn't know what He wanted me to do. Growing up, I was not the most talented kid in school. I never excelled at anything requiring a skill. I assumed I couldn't serve Jesus both because I was a terrible singer and because my lack of athletic skills would certainly cause the church softball team to lose. So as an adult woman, all that was in my hand was a deep love for Jesus, coupled with a passion for His Word. Then one day my pastor called and said, "Marian, we want you to teach a Bible study." I protested and offered up all the reasons why I couldn't do it. (Fear of public speaking was first on my list, quickly followed by a complete fear of failure!) But something in my heart told me that this call was from the Lord. I went to my mentor, and she said, "Marian, you have everything needed to serve Him well. Stay humble. It is not about you. All you need, you already have in your hand—a passionate love for Jesus and His Word." With this encouragement, I said, "Yes!"

The funny thing is, I didn't even know that teaching was one of my spiritual gifts. I didn't know because I'd never used the gift. Even though there was still so much for me to learn, I stepped out in faith and began to use what God put in my hand. Honestly, I was so nervous that I nearly threw up before each lesson. But those early days of teaching Bible study were the foundation for the call on my life that still continues today.

What about you? What has the Lord placed in your hand?

Perhaps you're a mom and "in your hand" is a carpool full of kiddos. Or maybe you're a college student and "in your hand" is a dorm of women who don't know Jesus. Perhaps you are working in an office filled with nonbelievers who are desperate for the hope and joy you've found in Jesus. Whether you are eighteen or ninety-eight, the Lord has placed something in your hand for His glory.

Today we've considered that God has called each of us to "go and make disciples." As the body of Christ, we share one Holy Spirit, but we are given a variety of different gifts. The best way to discover yours is by stepping up to serve in your local church. If you love kids, then volunteer to help in the children's ministry. If you are passionate about teaching God's Word, then volunteer to lead a small group. As you serve, your spiritual gifts will become evident. Just give Jesus your "yes" (Romans 12:1), and He will use your life for His glory.

Prayer

In the space below, connect with God using your own words:

DAY 3: CALLED TO SPIRITUAL MATURITY

Focal Point

Begin today's study by reading Ephesians 4:14-16.

I wear many hats: wife, author, friend, daughter, Bible teacher, and momma. I've been gigging at this motherhood thing for almost three years now. Motherhood is the most life-altering, heart-wrenching, joy-filled, bone-weary job I've ever known. *I love every minute of it*, although I was initially terrified at the prospect.

I vividly recall during pregnancy being gripped with fear at the incredible responsibility that would soon be placed in my arms. The thought of raising a child and not totally screwing her up freaked me out. I told a friend of mine, "I feel more capable of being air-dropped into a war-torn country and finding my way out in the midst of a gun battle than I do in raising a baby."

I've always been prone to the dramatic.

God doesn't wait for us to be ready to stretch us. I've learned that He equips us in the midst of the mess. Now that I'm well into this motherhood thing, I've discovered it is not something we learn from books; this is a hands-on, learn-as-we-go, trial-and-error business.

I'll be honest, every time when we take Sydney to her pediatrician checkup, I walk into the doctor's office expecting her to give me a lollipop and a sticker because (a) my child is in one piece, and (b) I am still in one piece. I kid, but seriously. The baby gets shots, and we get nothing for all the sleepless nights and ceaseless prayers asking Jesus to take the wheel.

The best thing about those pediatrician appointments was learning the developmental milestones Sydney should have achieved at each particular stage. For a child, growth is the expectation. Over a few short months, babies mature from helpless little eight-pound infants to twenty-eight-pound toddlers bent on demolishing every single thing in their path. As I've watched in wonder as my little girl has matured from infancy to the fantastic adventure of toddlerhood, I can't help thinking about spiritual maturity. Just as good parents are thrilled to see their children develop new skills, so our heavenly Father delights as we grow and mature in our faith.

The Bible is clear that spiritual maturity is the expectation (not the exception) for all Christians. Just as a baby is born and then begins to grow, so we too are "born again" into God's family, and then we start to mature as children of God. Although this is the expectation, often many Christians get stuck and don't progress in their faith.

Today's Focal Point is about growing in spiritual maturity. Let's look at these verses in context by reading all of Ephesians 4:1-16.

What do you observe by reading verses 14-16 in context (what you didn't know before)?

> *God doesn't wait for us to be ready to stretch us.*

> *The new life of Christ that is created in us at our salvation is meant to flourish and mature.*

As a result of the call to walk in a manner worthy of Christ and the call to use our spiritual gifts to build up the church (what we studied yesterday), verse 14 states

"we will no longer be _____ " (NIV).

Jesus used the term "born again" to describe the supernatural work of regeneration that occurs by the Holy Spirit when we believe in Him (John 3:1-16). That person is made alive with Christ (Ephesians 2:1-10). As a result, persons who are young in their faith are likened to an infant (some translations use the word *children*). They are a child of God, but they still need to mature in faith and grow in Christlikeness.

Friend, spiritual growth is the expectation we find in Scripture. In God's plan, the new life of Christ that is created in us at our salvation is meant to flourish and mature. Just as an infant is nourished and grows into a toddler, then into a child, and then into a teenager who, thankfully, becomes an adult, so too a child of God also matures.

How did Paul characterize the state of spiritual "infants"? What can happen to their faith? (Ephesians 4:14)

> Rather, speaking the truth in love, we are to grow up in every way into him who is the head, into Christ.
> *EPHESIANS 4:15 ESV*

Tossed around and blown by waves doesn't sound fun at all. So, we are called to mature from infancy. Fill in the blanks below according to verse 15:

"Rather, speaking the _____ in love, we will _____."

Scripture outlines some "spiritual milestones" in 2 Peter 1:3-11 that should increase in our lives if we are indeed children of God. These milestones are not a legalistic checklist whereby we strive to perfect ourselves. Instead, these qualities are the evidence that we belong to Jesus and are spiritually maturing.

Read 2 Peter 1:3-11 and answer the following:
What has God's divine power given to us? (v. 3)

List the qualities that a child of God should progress in as she matures. (vv. 5-7)

Time for self-evaluation. How is God currently maturing you?

What do these qualities accomplish in a believer's life? (v. 8)

But we all, with unveiled face, beholding as in a mirror the glory of the Lord, are being transformed into the same image from glory to glory, just as from the Lord, the Spirit.

2 CORINTHIANS 3:18 NASB

This self-evaluation is not meant to heap shame upon us but to help us honestly ask ourselves if we are indeed growing in maturity. Here is the hope for every child of God: "God is the one who began this good work in you, and I am certain that he won't stop before it is complete on the day that Christ Jesus returns" (Philippians 1:6 CEV). As we surrender more and more to the power of the Holy Spirit and grow in our knowledge of Jesus, the result is maturity. Just as Paul writes in 2 Corinthians 3:18, as we behold Jesus, we become like Jesus!

Just as my daughter Sydney no longer behaves like an infant but has progressed to a thriving and busy toddler, born-again believers should mature spiritually beyond their initial conversion. Incidentally, I've met teenagers who are more spiritually mature than some older adults I know. Spiritual maturity is not about age; it is 100 percent about growing in our relationship with God. And I assume that if you've stuck with me this far, then you are someone who wants to mature in her faith. I do too, friend!

So how do we do it? How do we grow in spiritual maturity? Here are three ways outlined in God's Word.

Like newborn babies, long for the pure milk of the word, so that by it you may grow in respect to salvation.

1 PETER 2:2 NASB

1. Consume the Word of God.

Here we are told that we grow in our faith by drinking the "pure milk of the word [of God]." This analogy is one I've witnessed with my own eyes. Infants are fed a diet of only milk for months, and their tiny fingers and toes and limbs begin to grow, stretch, and develop from simply drinking milk! It is not a coincidence that the Bible describes itself as the "pure milk" for our spiritual growth. For a believer to mature in her faith, she must feed herself the Word of God on a daily basis. It is not enough to go to church once a week. That would be like eating a meal on Sunday and then starving for the remainder of the week. We must daily feed ourselves the Word of God if we expect to grow and mature in our faith.

Bible studies such as this one are excellent tools for nourishing your soul. I also would recommend a daily Bible reading plan. There are numerous free ones available online. I offer one on my free app (This Redeemed Life) that provides an easy way to read or listen to Scripture each day. With the convenience of technology, you can listen to God's Word while washing dishes, commuting to work, or even jogging at the gym. As we take in the nourishment of God's truth, we are strengthened by its power and transformed from the inside out (Romans 12:2).

How can you better prioritize your consumption of God's Word?

²⁴And let us consider how we may spur one another on toward love and good deeds, ²⁵not giving up meeting together, as some are in the habit of doing, but encouraging one another—and all the more as you see the Day approaching.

HEBREWS 10:24-25 NIV

2. Cultivate Christ-centered community.

I can testify that nothing in the world has fostered spiritual maturity in my life more than surrounding myself with other Christ-followers who love the Lord and who desire to live for His glory. One of my very first prayers after I began to follow Jesus was for the gift of Christian friends. Over the past two decades, I've seen God answer that prayer above and beyond all I could ask or imagine. He has richly provided community. I believe God answered that prayer so abundantly because He knows the importance of it.

Notice how the Hebrews passage says that by gathering together with others who love Jesus, we "spur one another on toward love and good deeds." This is spiritual maturity. When we surround ourselves with a Christ-centered community, then we invite accountability, we are challenged to know God more, and we have relationships with people who will pray for us when trials or temptations occur. Indeed, we are better together.

How has a Christ-centered community (or lack of one) affected your spiritual growth?

Who is "spurring you on" toward love and good deeds?
(If you have trouble answering this question, write a prayer to God asking for Christian community.)

Spiritual growth is not up to us, nor accomplished by our own power.

3. Ask for help.

Last week we learned that we are the temple of the Holy Spirit. Since God's Spirit indwells us, He is the One who empowers us to grow in Christlikeness. We also learned that we can come to God in prayer, asking for His spirit to increase in us. Here, those two powerful concepts come together.

Jesus called the Holy Spirit our "Helper." He is the one who comes alongside us and helps us in our weaknesses. The Spirit transforms us from the inside out to act, to think, and to love like Jesus. As we see an area in which we need to mature, we ask the Holy Spirit to take the lead and do the work of transformation.

For example, when I read the "spiritual milestones" listed in 2 Peter 1:3-11, I stop and ask the Holy Spirit to mature me in each of these areas, especially the ones I find lacking in my life such as self-control. (Can I get an "amen"?) Thankfully, spiritual growth is not up to us, nor accomplished by our own power. But it *is* up to us to ask the Holy Spirit for help and to yield to His power as He works within us.

Now it's your turn. In what aspect of your life do you need to ask the Holy Spirit to help you grow?

The Helper, the Holy Spirit, whom the Father will send in my name, will teach you everything and make you remember all that I have told you.
JOHN 14:26 GNT

The Big Picture

"The Christian life from start to finish is based upon this principle of utter dependence upon the Lord Jesus."

WATCHMAN NEE[5]

What an amazing day we've had in God's Word together. I pray you're encouraged that God is not finished with you! I sure am. The same Holy Spirit who gives us a new life in Christ is the One who transforms us to become more like Jesus. Looking back over two decades of walking with Jesus, I know from experience that God uses His Word, His people, and His Spirit to mature us into Christlikeness. Why does He do this amazing work of transformation? Because we are His masterpiece, created in Christ Jesus to display His glory!

Prayer

In the space below, connect with God using your own words:

DAY 4: CALLED TO LAY ASIDE THE OLD SELF

Focal Point

Begin today's study by reading Ephesians 4:17-24.

I'm a Texas girl through and through. I love horses, chips and salsa at every meal, country music, and beautiful sunsets. However, there is one thing I don't love about my home state—August, when those who call it home feel like we are living on the sun. Our grass is crispy brown. We can bake cookies in our parked cars. I'm not exaggerating when I tell you that it is 106 degrees at 8:00 p.m. As I like to say, "It is blazing saddles hot outside!"

For some insane reason, I thought it would be a good idea to reboot my fitness routine during the hottest month of the year. I set a goal to run a 10K in December, hoping this would motivate me to get back in shape. Unfortunately, this impulse ignited during the blistering heat and suffocating humidity of August.

I thought running at 5:00 p.m. would be cooler than midday, but boy was I wrong. I tortured myself with just two miles, and by the time I returned to my car, I was utterly drenched. My face was bright red, my clothes were dripping sweat, and I smelled horrific.

The first thing I did when I returned home was rip off those wet, stinky clothes and take a good shower. I'm telling you that was the best shower of my life. When I stepped out, I put on my clean, fluffy white bathrobe and poured myself sparkling ice water. I felt like a new woman.

Now, I have a question for you: how crazy would it have been if I picked up those filthy clothes and put them back on my freshly cleaned body? The shower would have been pointless, right? This, my friend, is the spiritual analogy given us in the remainder of Ephesians 4. For those of us who have been redeemed and made righteous by Jesus, we are called to "lay aside" the old (stinky, rotten, gross) behavior of our former manner of living and "put on" the new life of Christ. Let's dive into today's Focal Point and discover what we are called to "lay aside."

Look again at Ephesians 4:17-24, and write your own paraphrase of verse 17.

In the New American Standard Bible, we read, "So this I say, and affirm together with the Lord." The Greek word used for "affirm" refers to a courtroom witness affirming if a statement is true or false. Here, Paul affirms that His words are from Jesus. These aren't merely helpful hints or tips to live your best life but words that carry the authority of Jesus regarding how a Christian should live in this world.

Read John 8:12. How did Jesus say those who followed Him would walk?

> *Our lifestyle should be one that increasingly reflects God's holiness, love, and goodness.*

The Big Picture

Gentile: *This word was used to denote those who were not Jewish and thus not included in God's covenant relationship with the people of Israel. Paul made it clear that God's grace and salvation had been extended to Gentiles as well as to Jews, opening the way for all people, through Christ, to have a relationship with God. For the Jews of Jesus' time, Gentiles were religious outsiders. Today we often use terms such as "non-Christian" or "nonbeliever" in a similar way.*

Now back to our Focal Point. What command is given in verse 17?

Recall that Ephesians 4:1 says we are called to walk in a manner "worthy of Christ." Throughout the New Testament, the word *walk* is often used to denote one's manner of living. As a Christ-follower, who has been redeemed from sin and darkness, our call is to no longer walk in that old lifestyle. I'm not saying we will never sin or be tempted by it, but our lifestyle should be one that increasingly reflects God's holiness, love, and goodness. Our walk should reveal the transformation that has occurred in our hearts because of the gospel. Therefore, today's Focal Point calls us to lay aside our old manner of living just as we would dirty clothing.

Read Ephesians 4:17-19. How does Paul describe the walk (or lifestyle) of Gentiles?

Their thinking (v. 17):

Their understanding, and the condition of their hearts (v. 18):

Their character (v. 19):

Look back at Ephesians 2:1-3. What similarities do you see?

As a little girl, I spent much of my childhood on my grandmother's small farm in East Texas. Her barn was home to horses, and the pond next to her house was the territory of the meanest ducks you've ever seen. In addition to this menagerie, there were a handful of dogs, who barked at cars and slept on the front porch. Last but not least, she owned a little pot-bellied pig. Over time, this little guy got caught up in the wrong crowd (so to speak). Little piggy started barking at cars, chasing cats, and pretty much living just like his four-legged companions the dogs.

While a funny scene to behold, this same danger faces us as Christ-followers. When surrounded by those who don't love or follow Jesus, we are tempted to conform to worldly thinking and behavior—which seems normal to nonbelievers—rather than the way of Christ. For this reason, we are warned of the perils of living like those who don't know Christ: because they live "in the futility of their mind" (v. 17 NASB).

This week in my Bible reading I found myself in Ecclesiastes, which was written by King Solomon and is a fascinating look at the word *futility*. This word, also translated "vanity," refers to anything momentary, empty, and lacking in substance. Solomon testifies that he tried to find life, pleasure, and satisfaction through knowledge, wealth, entertainment, and women. He built lavish houses and acquired vast riches, but all was "futility." None of it brought true fulfillment.

I know this struggle all too well. Before Christ, I chased after all the things the world said would bring me happiness—men, success, beauty, popularity, and even a little bit of fame. *Futile* is an excellent word to describe my old life. There is never enough food, alcohol, sex, shopping, or time in the spotlight to fill the God-shaped hole in our souls. Why? We are created by God for a relationship with Him, and until we turn to Jesus and find real life, all the rest is meaningless.

Here the apostle Paul describes Gentiles as living in the "futility of their mind" because they hope something of this world will satisfy the deep cravings of their souls. In 1 John 2:15-17 (in the margin), this futility is described as living according to "the world's ways" (v. 15 The Message). The world gives us a prescription for happiness that is centered upon living for self and momentary pleasures.

This teaching echoes Paul's plea to us in Ephesians 4 to no longer walk like the Gentiles who do not know God.

What about you? How have you experienced the "futility" of living for this world?

15-17 Don't love the world's ways. Don't love the world's goods. Love of the world squeezes out love for the Father. Practically everything that goes on in the world—wanting your own way, wanting everything for yourself, wanting to appear important—has nothing to do with the Father. It just isolates you from him. The world and all its wanting, wanting, wanting is on the way out—but whoever does what God wants is set for eternity.

1 JOHN 2:15-17
THE MESSAGE

So whether you eat or drink or whatever you do, do it all for the glory of God.

1 CORINTHIANS 10:31 NIV

What is something you've chased after, hoping it would fulfill you, that only resulted in more emptiness?

A life of futility is also characterized as one without true purpose. The believer in Christ understands that she has been redeemed for a purpose—to live for the glory to God. Consequently, as God's masterpiece, all that is done in this life should be for His glory (see 1 Corinthians 10:31).

How can you resist a life of futility and live for God's glory today?

As God's masterpiece, all that is done in this life should be for His glory.

Verse 18 in our Focal Point talks about hardened hearts. A hardened heart describes the spiritual condition of someone who does not know God (vividly illustrated in Ephesians 2:1-3). But a Christian who loves Jesus still faces a real danger: our hearts can grow hard toward the Lord. How could this happen? This occurs if we willfully choose to disobey God's commands and walk in darkness. This would be like me putting on those putrid running clothes after taking a shower!

Sin begins with temptation, and when we yield to that temptation repeatedly, it forms a callus around the heart. Just as a callus was once a tender spot on the skin that grew tough, so, too, our hearts can turn from soft to callous toward the Lord. The Holy Spirit convicts us to lead us back to the Lord, but if we ignore the conviction, our hearts grow harder. The result is that we lose the intimacy of relationship we can experience with Jesus.

I'm praying for each of us that the Holy Spirit would reveal any ways our hearts have grown hard toward God. *Repentance* is not a word we use much anymore, but it is one of the most beautiful words in Scripture. Repent means to turn and face a new direction. If we've been walking in a particular sin, then repentance means we turn away from that sin and embrace Jesus again. This turn is the act of responding to the conviction of the Holy Spirit, agreeing with God about the sin, and receiving the grace He offers.

In the parable of the prodigal son, who runs away from his father and squanders his inheritance, there is a moment when he is covered in pig slop and comes to his senses, deciding to run home. This turning and returning is repentance. Our Father waits for us with open arms when we recognize our sin and return to the arms of grace.

Read the story of the prodigal son in Luke 15:11-32.

What do you imagine the prodigal son had to "lay aside" before the father clothed him in a new robe?

Now look back to Luke 15:10. What is the response in heaven when someone repents?

> *Our Father waits for us with open arms when we recognize our sin and return to the arms of grace.*

Resisting worldliness and repenting of sin are both embodied in Ephesians 4:17-23 with the call to lay aside the old self. Our "old self" was once enslaved to the world's way of selfish thinking, and our hearts were once hard toward God because of sin. But now as Christ-followers, we live for the glory of God. For this reason, today's Focal Point closes with a strong reminder of what Christ has done for us and what our daily practice must be if we are to walk worthy of our calling.

Turn again to Ephesians 4:17-24.

What are we called to do in verse 22?

What are called to do in verse 23?

What words are used to describe the "new self" in verse 24?

Friend, to lay aside the old self is a daily choice that flows from a heart that says, "Jesus is better!" Honestly, the times when I do walk in the "old self" I feel gross (no one likes wearing dirty clothes!). I can feel my joy diminished and my sensitivity to God's presence lessened.

Taste and see that
the LORD is good;
blessed is the
one who takes
refuge in him.

PSALM 34:8 NIV

Just as we walk in our closets and pick out an outfit for the day, so we make a daily decision to lay aside the old and put on the new. Today, I choose to lay aside my old self and put on Christ because I have tasted and seen that the Lord is good! Friend, I pray the same for you. I hope your motivation to live for God's glory is a response to His goodness and grace in your life. I pray you respond to Jesus' lavish love with a surrendered heart that longs to show the world the goodness of your God!

Prayer

In the space below, connect with God using your own words:

DAY 5: PUT ON THE NEW SELF

Focal Point

Begin today's study by reading Ephesians 4:25-32.

One of the most faith-building stories in the Gospels is the miraculous moment when Jesus raised Lazarus from the dead. If you are unfamiliar with this miracle, I want to share a few of the highlights.

Jesus was close friends with a man named Lazarus and his two sisters, Mary and Martha. Throughout His ministry, Jesus would often stay in their home during his travels to and from Jerusalem. Just a short time before Jesus was crucified, word reached Him that Lazarus was extremely sick. The sisters knew Jesus had the power to heal, so they sent a messenger to beg Him to come quickly. By the time Jesus finally arrived, it was too late. Lazarus was dead and buried in the tomb for four days. Let's pick up the story in Scripture and discover how this perfectly illustrates today's Focal Point.

Read John 11:17-46.

What did Martha say to Jesus when he arrived? (vv. 21-22)

What was Jesus' response? (v. 23)

What promise did Jesus make to Martha? (vv. 25-26)

How did Jesus react to Lazarus's death? (v. 35)

Describe the miracle Jesus performed. (vv. 38-45)

What specific command did Jesus give? (v. 44)

In biblical times, the burial process included anointing the body with spices and wrapping it in linen cloths. It's vital to note that Jesus immediately commanded Lazarus be released from his graveclothes. Why? Because death attire was not fitting for the living. How strange would it have been for Lazarus to go back to work or to a meal still wearing the linen graveclothes? The same bears true for us. Ephesians declares that each person who responds to Jesus is brought from death to life (see Ephesians 2:1-4). Now we are alive in Christ and called to lay aside the old graveclothes of our sinful nature. We take off the "old self" (sinful attitudes and actions) and put on our "new self," the life of Christ.

Look back again at Ephesians 4:24. What words are used to describe the "new self"?

Therefore, if anyone is in Christ, the new creation has come: The old has gone, the new is here!

2 CORINTHIANS 5:17 NIV

The new self is the likeness of God, created in righteousness, holiness, and truth. Friend, this is who we are—not who we are trying to become. In Christ, we are 100 percent righteous. Why? Because Jesus is pure holiness and we are "in Him." Grasping this truth is fundamental to our walk. We aren't striving to become more holy; we are laying aside our old self to walk in our new nature.

Read 2 Corinthians 5:17 in the margin. What do you discover about your old self?

For by these He has granted to us His previous and magnificent promises, so that by them you may become partakers of the divine nature, having escaped the corruption that is in the world by lust.

2 PETER 1:4 NASB

Read 2 Peter 1:4 in the margin. What have we become partakers of?

A glorious transformation occurred at salvation. Yesterday we looked at the call to "lay aside" our old self from a general perspective, and in today's text we get into the nitty-gritty of what we specifically are called to take off and put on.

Let's dig into Ephesians 4:25-32 and briefly discover the things we as believers are called to take off. These are actions or attitudes that are consistent with our old, dead, sinful nature.

Take off _____. (v. 25)

Take off _____. (v. 26)

Take off _____. ((v. 28)

Take off _____. (v. 29)

Take off _____, _____,

_____, _____,

_____, and _____. (v. 31)

While each of these merits a full study, for the remainder of our time together today we will dive into two behaviors we are called to take off. Both are practical and relational in nature, and I find that most of us are tempted to walk in our "old self" in these areas.

Take Off Falsehood

Before I began following Jesus, I was a liar—and a really good one. I felt no conviction about it. I could look someone in the eye and tell a tall tale. But when I surrendered my life to Christ and experienced the forgiveness of my sins (past, present, and future), I discovered that I couldn't continue to practice this same sin as I did before.

One night I was at a dinner party when everyone began sharing stories. I began to tell a story, and as I talked, the old habit of lying kicked into gear. Soon the story became more and more exaggerated until many of the details were flat-out lies. I left that dinner party and drove home to my apartment. When I sat down on my bed to read my Bible, I felt deep conviction. The Holy Spirit didn't shame me or condemn me, but He spoke directly to my heart and said, "Marian, you lied."

I had a choice. I could harden my heart to God's voice, or I could repent of the sin. By God's grace, I repented. I went back to where a few friends were still gathered and said these words, "I lied, and God won't let me lie anymore because that's not who I am." I can still feel the heaviness that lifted off me. I can recall the power of the Holy Spirit that surged through me as I yielded to the conviction and confessed my sin. Today I can tell you with a grateful heart that I do not struggle with lying anymore. I took off that old, dead clothing and put on the new nature of Christ.

True repentance required more than merely confessing that I lied. I had to take a deep look in my heart and ask why. The Bible speaks of roots and fruit. While I could easily identify the fruit of my behavior (a false statement), I needed to take the next step and search out the root (why I was tempted to lie).

Lying is a temptation we all face from time to time, whether we want to impress someone or we want to cover up a mistake. Shame was the root of lying in my life. Shame says we must cover ourselves in order to be found acceptable. I felt I needed to lie to cover my shortcomings or to hide my imperfections. As I brought this root to Jesus, He showed me that I didn't need to hide in shame because He makes me fully accepted. I don't need to try to make myself more lovable or perfect in the eyes of people; He has done that

> *The more we come to believe who we are in Christ, the less power that the temptation to lie has on us.*

work. The more we come to believe who we are in Christ, the less power that the temptation to lie has on us.

When are you tempted to lie? (Keep in mind, a lie can be not keeping a commitment or flat-out dishonesty.)

Now, go past the fruit. What is the root of this behavior?

How have you experienced conviction similar to my story? Have you ever felt the Holy Spirit calling you to lay aside an old sinful practice?

Take Off Anger

Another characteristic of our old self that we must take off is a bad temper. The Bible doesn't tell us that we shouldn't feel angry, but it is important to handle our emotions properly. We must not allow anger to fester into pride, hatred, or self-righteousness. One commentary notes this about anger:

> If vented thoughtlessly, anger can hurt others and destroy relationships. If kept inside, it can cause us to become bitter and destroy us from within. Paul tells us to deal with our anger immediately in a way that builds relationships rather than destroys them. If we nurse our anger, we will give Satan an opportunity to divide us. Anger must be dealt with as quickly as possible. Used correctly, anger can motivate us to right a wrong, redress a grievance, correct an injustice.[6]

We are called to lay aside anger like a dirty garment because this sin can lead to much destruction. How do we do this? I'll be honest, in my flesh I can be prone to anger. Over the years I've taken various personality tests, and each states that I have a high desire for justice. When a situation feels like an injustice, it strikes a chord and I feel deeply passionate about the situation. This passion can be channeled for good to fight against injustices, but in my flesh these reactions can lead to sin. I've learned I must take these emotions to God to respond rightly.

When I stop and pray the Holy Spirit helps me get to the root of my anger. Discovering *why* I am angry enables me to respond rightly rather than rashly. Just this week I was upset with my husband. When I stopped, walked away, and asked the Lord to help me handle my anger, Jesus showed me that the root of it was fear.

I confessed my fear to God and then to my husband. We forgave each other and enjoyed a great weekend. I've learned through my own experiences that to "lay aside" anger means we must pray, process, and proceed in a relationship with the power of God. Keep in mind, there is an enemy at work who wants to "steal, kill, and destroy." The devil loves it when a child of God walks in her old sinful nature. While he can't do one single thing about our eternal destiny if we are in Christ, he can still wreak havoc in our personal relationships when we indulge in sin. This is what Paul refers to when he says, "Do not let the sun go down while you are still angry, and do not give the devil a foothold" (Ephesians 4:26-27 NIV).

Bible teacher Warren Wiersbe explains, "Satan hates God and God's people, and when he finds a believer with the sparks of anger in his heart, he fans those sparks, adds fuel to the fire, and does a great deal of damage to God's people and God's church."[7]

Can you think of a time when reacting in anger only added fuel to a fire? If so, write about it briefly:

Read today's Focal Point, Ephesians 4:25-32, again. If you are comfortable writing in your Bible, circle every occurrence of "do not."

> *Just as we choose each day what clothing we will wear, so we make a choice to walk in our old sinful nature or to walk in the nature of Christ.*

Do Not Grieve the Holy Spirit

The human will is the place of decision. God gives us free will to make choices. Just as we choose each day what clothing we will wear, so we make a choice to walk in our old sinful nature or to walk in the nature of Christ. Ephesians 4 closes with the warning that our choices can grieve the Holy Spirit. This is crucial to grasp: the Holy Spirit is a person. He is not merely a force or a power but the third person of the Trinity, who has emotions. When a child of God chooses to live in a manner unworthy of Christ, then we hurt God's heart. Let's keep in mind that a decision to indulge in sin or walk in darkness will grieve God's heart because He paid the ultimate price to redeem us from sin's captivity.

Finally, after calling those who practice stealing to take off this sinful habit, Paul again addresses issues of the heart that affect our personal relationships—specifically our words. (Ouch!) Warren Wiersbe notes, "Our lips should speak that which builds up (Col. 4:6; Ps. 141:3). Corruption from the lips only means that there is corruption in the heart."[8]

Can you think of a time when your words were used to tear down rather than build up?

Here is the good news: If we've grieved God's Spirit, we can turn and restore fellowship again. The Holy Spirit doesn't shame us but calls us back home to the Father's heart so that we can experience restored intimacy with God. Acts 3:19 encourages us with these words: "Repent, then, and turn to God, so that he will forgive your sins" (GNT).

Today we've looked at a few examples of the old graveclothes that we are to lay aside once we experience new life in Jesus. This vivid imagery is meant to encourage us each day to choose Jesus. As God's masterpiece, we must choose to wear the righteousness of Jesus and walk in His love. As Ephesians 4:32 tell us, "Be kind to one another, tenderhearted, forgiving one another, as God in Christ forgave you." I can't think of any words more fitting or needed in our world today. As Christ-followers, we need to exhibit the kindness and forgiveness that God has shown to us in Christ. Just think what a difference your light could make in the darkness that surrounds you if you choose to heed this call today. Let's be kind. Let's be tenderhearted to others—even with those with whom we don't see eye to eye, and especially with those who've wronged us. In doing so, the world will see God's masterpiece of grace and love in us!

Prayer

In the space below, connect with God using your own words:

SESSION 5: VIDEO VIEWER GUIDE

Ephesians 5:1-2 – Imitate God

We _____ to Jesus to be saved, but we
_____ at Jesus to be transformed.

We become what we behold.

1 John 1:5 – God is light
Isaiah 42:6-7 – A light to the nations
Isaiah 60:1-3 – Your light has come
John 1:1-10 – The Word and the life, the light of all
John 12:35-36 – Believe in the light
Matthew 5:14-16 – You are the light of the world
Ephesians 5:1-2 – Be imitators of God
Ephesians 5:8-15 – You are light in the Lord

1. *We display the light of Christ by living a life of*
    _____.

2. *We display the light of Christ by living a life of*
    _____.

Forgiveness never means that something that was wrong is okay.
Forgiveness is releasing another's debt to God.

WEEK 5: THE SPIRIT-FILLED LIFE

Overview

Jesus called His followers the Light of the World. Light has the power to illuminate, heal, reveal, and guide. Each of these words describes our calling as God's masterpiece—we are to shine a spotlight on Jesus Christ. But this amazing declaration begs the question—*how*? How do we illuminate the darkness? How do we live in this world yet not conform to it? How do we reflect the beauty and glory of Christ to those around us? These questions are the focus of our study this week as we learn to live for His glory!

DAY 1: WALK IN LOVE

Focal Point

Begin today's study by reading Ephesians 5:1-2.

One of my most cherished memories as a momma occurred at our church when my daughter was just eleven months old. (Confession, I was one of those clingy moms who kept her kid in big church for the first year of her life when a perfectly good nursery was just steps away.) When Sydney was an infant, I wore her across my chest in a baby carrier until she grew too big for it, which happened faster than I could blink! Then I switched to her stroller and stood at the back of the sanctuary, pushing her back and forth to keep her quiet. Finally, as she grew older and more restless, I just held her on my hip, and we swayed together as I praised Jesus.

Week by week, we worshiped God. I didn't realize it at the time, but my baby was watching. Then one day when she was nearly a year old, I saw the sweetest thing in the world—Sydney raised her chubby little hand in praise. What was she doing? She was imitating her momma. She'd watched me worship Jesus with my hands held high so many times; so when the music began to play, she simply did what she saw me doing. That moment solidified the sacredness of motherhood. My daughter was watching my life and would be influenced by it—for better or for worse.

In what ways do you resemble the person who raised you as a child? (What features, gestures, or quirks did you inherit or pick up?)

Children imitate their parents. The expression "Like father, like son" testifies to this reality. It's surreal watching my bonus-boys with my husband. I see Justin's mannerisms and so much of his personality in both of them. One has his laugh and the other his walk. This is the message we learn today in Ephesians—as God's children, we should look and act like Him.

Ephesians 5:1 begins with an important word—*therefore*. The word *therefore* serves as a bridge that connects two thoughts. Here the apostle Paul links what he has taught previously in chapter 4 with what is about to come in chapter 5. This bridge links the call to "walk worthy of our calling" with the idea that we are "beloved children" of God. Whenever I'm teaching the Bible, I like to remind people to stop and ask this question: what's the *therefore* there for? Now let's answer that question together.

Let's begin by putting this verse in context. Read all of Ephesians 4:1–5:2 and then complete the following:

If you are comfortable writing in your Bible, draw a small arrow from the word **therefore** *in verse 5:1 back to the previous verse, Ephesians 4:32.*

Now let's connect the bridge so we can fully appreciate what we are called to do. Write Ephesians 4:32 below:

What stands out to you as you read today's Focal Point, Ephesians 5:1-2, in context?

Marvel at the fact that you are God's beloved child. He fights for you. He delights in you. He loves you. I've often heard that the most loving people are the ones who know they are loved. With that in mind, let's take a look at how Jesus linked our identity as God's beloved children with the call to love others:

43"You have heard that it was said, 'Love your neighbor and hate your enemy.' 44But I tell you, love your enemies and pray for those who persecute you, 45that you may be children of your Father in heaven. He causes his sun to rise on the evil and the good, and sends rain on the righteous and the unrighteous. 46If you love those who love you, what reward will you get? Are not even the tax collectors doing that?47And if you greet only your own people, what are you doing more than others? Do not even pagans do that?48 Be perfect, therefore, as your heavenly Father is perfect.
MATTHEW 5:43-48 NIV

What does Jesus command us to do in verse 44?

Why does Jesus call us to love our neighbor? (vv. 45 and 48)

We love because we are loved. As we proceed in our study of Ephesians, it proves essential to ground the reason for our changed behavior in our changed identity. We don't love others in order to earn favor with God; we love others because He first loved us. All Christian ethics spring from a Christ-centered identity. Because I am the "beloved" I am called to walk in love.

Read John 13:34-35. What new command does Christ give to us?

What did Jesus say that love proves to the world?

Read 1 John 4:7-12. What two things are true of the person who loves? (v. 7)

Fill in the blank from verse 8. "God is _____."

How do verses 9-10 define love?

What is the right response to God's love for us? (v. 11)

It's one thing to know the Bible bids us to love others and quite a different thing to know how to do it. Love is complicated. Sometimes it's downright messy. How do I love my enemy? How do I love the person who is different from me? How do I love the person who doesn't seem to deserve it? How do I love the person who rejects my love? *How do we love like God loves?*

To Love, We Must Abide in Christ

I'm going to be honest. There are people in my life I'm called to love whom I don't even like sometimes. But my feelings have nothing to do with my obedience to God's call. I am called to love others with the same lavish love extended to me by God. But how? Over and over again, I must come back to Jesus' simple words: "Apart from Me, you can do nothing" (John 15:5).

Jesus spoke these words to His disciples on the eve of His death. As Jesus progressed closer to his crucifixion, He intentionally prepared His followers for life after His resurrection, when they would experience connection with Him through the Holy Spirit instead of through His physical presence. To illustrate this Spirit-

Abiding in Christ is our lifeline in the midst of a world that demands far too much of us.

empowered life, Jesus took them to a vineyard to illustrate the dynamic relationship between a vine and its branches.

Read John 15:1-14. As you read, personalize this passage by saying your name wherever you see the word you.

With what does Jesus compare Himself? (v. 1)

Write verse 4 below:

What is the result of abiding? (v. 5)

What does Jesus promise in verse 7?

What is the result of abiding in Christ? (v. 8)

What does Jesus say is true of you in verse 9?

*How does Jesus define **great love** in verse 13?*

The word *abide* (or *remain*) means "to stay connected." Just as a branch draws nutrients from the vine in order to grow and produce fruit, so too we draw the lifegiving supply of His Spirit when we abide in Jesus. Abiding in Jesus means we receive from Him our daily supply of love, peace, sanity, joy, patience, life, breath, and power. He wasn't kidding when He said, "Apart from Me you can do nothing" (John 15:5). Abiding is the key to the Christian life. In my own power, I can't love the person who irritates or infuriates me; I need Jesus' power to do the impossible.

This is not just a verse that we commit to memory; abiding in Christ is our power source. Abiding in Christ is our lifeline in the midst of a world that demands far too much of us. Abiding in Him is our ability to do what is impossible in the natural, because God's love is supernatural.

Read Galatians 5:22-23. What is produced in the life of a branch connected to the Vine?

Galatians 5:22 states that the fruit of the Holy Spirit is "love." This means that when we abide in Christ, then His Spirit will produce the godly character that is impossible in our own power. Remember, Jesus promised us in John 15:7 that whatever we ask Him to do, He will do it. This is a powerful promise for our daily lives; we can ask Jesus in a moment of need to love others through us. We may find ourselves in situations where love feels impossible; but when we stay connected to the Vine, then He will produce His love through us.

Now, let's take a look at one of the most famous passages in the Bible, 1 Corinthians 13. How is love defined in these verses?

After reflecting on the Bible's definition of love and the fact that we can't do it ourselves, whom do you need Jesus to love through you today?

To love, We Must Imitate Christ

The second way we fulfill the holy calling to love as God loves is by imitating Jesus! James M. Boice makes this amazing observation about the Greek text from Ephesians 5:1, which states, "Be imitators of God as beloved children."

> The word that our text translates "imitate" or "imitator" is *mimētai*, from which we get our English word "mimic." Mimic means to copy closely, to repeat another person's speech, actions, or behavior. That is what we are to do with God. We are to repeat his actions, echo his speech, duplicate his behavior. How can we do that if we do not

The Big Picture

"Do not waste time bothering whether you 'love' your neighbor; act as if you did. As soon as we do this we find one of the great secrets. When you are behaving as if you loved someone, you will presently come to love him."[1]

C. S. LEWIS,
MERE CHRISTIANITY

The more time we spend with Jesus, the more we will look like Jesus.

spend time with him? We cannot, because we will not even know what his behavior is. Spend time with God! Spend time with God in prayer. Spend time with God in Bible study. Spend time with God in worship. It is only by spending time with God that we become like God.[2]

Friend, the more time we spend with Jesus, the more we will look like Jesus. As I behold His heart in the Word and see how He reacts to those who hated Him, then I know how to respond to those who treat me unjustly. When I see how Jesus forgives, then I know how to forgive. When I watch how Jesus served, then I discover how I am to serve others. In beholding, we are becoming.

I pray today's study has encouraged you. At first the call to "imitate God" seems utterly impossible, but remember Jesus' words: "Apart from Me, you can do nothing"! Jesus empowers us to live a life that glorifies Him as we stay connected to Him. Day by day as we spend time with Jesus, we become more and more like Him. Just as my daughter mimics my voice, my gestures, and my walk, we too as God's children will learn to walk in love because He is love.

Prayer

In the space below, connect with God using your own words:

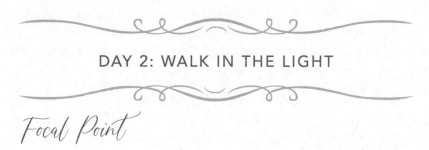

DAY 2: WALK IN THE LIGHT

Focal Point

Begin today's study by reading Ephesians 5:3-14.

The phrase "I pulled a Marian" means only one thing in my world. Someone, usually yours truly, has forgotten something. I like to think my forgetfulness is endearing, although I'm sure if you were to poll my closest buddies or my husband, they'd probably say they find it annoying at times. Thankfully, they extend me much grace as I repeatedly misplace my keys, phone, or Bible. Over the years, I've grown in self-acceptance and extremely fond of sticky notes. Let me share a moment when I forgot something extremely important.

To celebrate our high school graduation, I went on a Caribbean cruise with a few girlfriends. I saved my babysitting money all year long, and my parents made huge sacrifices to send me. The morning of the cruise, we drove hours from our small hometown to where we would board the ship. With images dancing through my head of the exotic locations that awaited me, I gleefully schlepped my luggage up to the boarding dock. Picture me now—sunglasses, cute summer dress, flip-flops, and a big hat. Sure, I looked ready, but in my excitement I forgot the most important item. No, not my swimsuit; I packed nine of those. Of course, I left the one thing that mattered most: my identification. You know, a passport, a driver's license, or even a birth certificate. I was sans any form of legit ID.

I was well past the age that a girl could just hop out of the country with a wink and a smile. Trust me, I tried it. Oh no, that pesky ship captain was oh-so-picky about proof of citizenship and such. Never fear friends, they were not leaving me behind! Thanks to my momma faxing my birth certificate, my best friend's prom picture displaying the two of us with our school's name, and a whole lot of persuasion by yours truly, I begged my way onto that cruise ship.

We behave how we believe.

151

[12]Giving joyful thanks to the Father, who has qualified you to share in the inheritance of his holy people in the kingdom of light. [13]For he has rescued us from the dominion of darkness and brought us into the kingdom of the Son he loves, [14]in whom we have redemption, the forgiveness of sins.

COLOSSIANS 1:12-14
NIV

Forgetting one's ID is a huge problem when it comes to international travel, yet this is not the only situation in which forgetting identification is problematic. When it comes to walking worthy of our calling as God's masterpiece, we must remember our identity in Christ.

Our God-Given Identity

Since "identity in Christ" is one of those phrases that is often thrown around but rarely explained, let's examine its meaning, which proves crucial to our study. Just as an identification card answers the question of who we are, so our God-given identity in Christ answers the same question. While my passport clearly identifies me as a citizen of the United States of America, God's Word clearly identifies me as a citizen of the kingdom of God (see Colossians 1:12-14). The Bible declares that with this new citizenship I have a new name, a new status, and a new purpose. And the same is true of you. We are no longer identified as we were before; now our identity is based upon who God says we are as His children.

Today our Focal Point drives an important point home about our God-given identity: we are children of light. We'll unpack exactly what this means; but before we get started, think about how important remembering our identity is. The reason is simple: we behave how we believe. Our actions and attitudes stem from our self-perception. So many people attempt to change their actions by sheer will or through discipline, not understanding that most of what we do is based upon our identity; therefore, we must start with recognizing who we are before we attempt to change what we do.

Now, let's discover the truth of our identity in Christ. Read Ephesians 5:1-15, and if you are comfortable marking in your Bible, circle every "you" in this passage.

Today's Focal Point begins by describing the lifestyle of those who walk in darkness. How is walking in darkness described in verses 3-7? What is listed as improper for God's holy people?

Ephesians 5:8-9 declares a change has occurred. Fill in the blanks with our new identity. (Note: This wording is based on the New International Version; other translations will vary.)

⁸*For you were once _____, but now you are _____ in the Lord. Live as _____ of _____* ⁹*for the fruit of the light consists in all goodness, righteousness and truth).* ¹⁰*and find out what pleases the Lord.*

What does verse 10 instruct us to do?

Now read Matthew 5:14-16 in the margin. What identity does Jesus give us?

How is this theme also emphasized in 1 John 1:5-9? How do these verses describe God? (v. 5)

What does verse 6 caution against?

Here's the tension we Christ-followers face this side of heaven: we are called the "light of world," yet we live in the midst of darkness that seeks to conform us to its agenda.

For you were once darkness, but now you are light in the Lord. Live as children of light.

EPHESIANS 5:8 NIV

¹⁴"You are the light of the world. A town built on a hill cannot be hidden. ¹⁵Neither do people light a lamp and put it under a bowl. Instead they put it on its stand, and it gives light to everyone in the house. ¹⁶In the same way, let your light shine before others, that they may see your good deeds and glorify your Father in heaven."

MATTHEW 5:14-16 NIV

153

Do not conform
to the pattern of
this world, but be
transformed by the
renewing of your
mind. Then you
will be able to test
and approve what
God's will is—his
good, pleasing
and perfect will.

ROMANS 12:2 NIV

Read Romans 12:2 in the margin. What does this verse say about the pressure to conform?

Conforming to the pattern of this world means we are walking in the darkness rather than in the light. How does this happen? We live in a world that is filled with selfishness, pride, lust, rage, materialism, and greed and that bombards us with messages designed to shape and mold our identity—and, consequently, our behavior—into its image. Because we see these visuals all day long, we think certain behaviors and attitudes are normal. Yet these are not "normal" for Christians because we are no longer citizens of the darkness but those who belong to the light. As Ephesians 5:3 (NIV) states, "But among you there must not be even a hint of sexual immorality, or of any kind of impurity, or of greed, because these are improper for God's holy people." In other words, these things may be celebrated by the culture around us, but not even a hint of the darkness should characterize a child of the light.

Take a look at 1 Thessalonians 4:3-5 in the margin. What is God's will for us as children of light?

³It is God's will
that you should
be sanctified: that
you should avoid
sexual immorality;
⁴that each of you
should learn to
control your own
body in a way
that is holy and
honorable, ⁵not in
passionate lust like
the pagans, who
do not know God.

1 THESSALONIANS
4:3-5 NIV

Keep in mind that Paul penned these words to people immersed in a culture of sexual perversion. It was common for men in this era to keep young boys as sex slaves. Orgies were practiced and widely accepted. The city of Ephesus was notorious for pagan idolatry and a sexual ethic that was not consistent with God's design for sex within the confines of covenant marriage. A chief sign that someone turned from pagan idolatry to embrace Christ as Lord was forsaking these pagan sexual practices.

Whenever one turns to Jesus and experiences His grace, then we comprehend that His commands concerning sex are good and meant to bless us. One of my favorite Scriptures that details God's design for sex was written by the apostle Paul to the church in Corinth. These believers were living in the midst of a culture very similar to Ephesus. See how beautifully God's glorious design is described:

> 16-20There's more to sex than mere skin on skin. Sex is as much spiritual mystery as physical fact. As written in Scripture, "The two become one." Since we want to become spiritually one with the Master, we must not pursue the kind of sex that avoids commitment and intimacy, leaving us more lonely than ever—the kind of sex that can never "become one." There is a sense in which sexual sins are different from all others. In sexual sin we violate the sacredness of our own bodies, these bodies that were made for God-given and God-modeled love, for "becoming one" with another. Or didn't you realize that your body is a sacred place, the place of the Holy Spirit? Don't you see that you can't live however you please, squandering what God paid such a high price for? The physical part of you is not some piece of property belonging to the spiritual part of you. God owns the whole works. So let people see God in and through your body.
>
> 1 CORINTHIANS 6:16-20 THE MESSAGE

How is God's design for sexual intimacy different from what the world advertises?

According to this Scripture, what does sexual sin violate?

Not even a hint of the darkness should characterize a child of the light.

155

What About Grace?

As I type these words, I can almost hear someone asking, "What about grace?" Friend, I hope you'll stick with me and see that fleeing from darkness and living according to God's will is the right response to God's amazing grace. Trust me, as I review the list of behaviors that characterize the kingdom of darkness, I wince. I don't have a stone to throw at anyone. My past was riddled with those sins. We all live in a world saturated with greed, pornography, and materialism and can easily be tempted to conform to our culture. The point of today's message isn't about striving for sinless perfection (Jesus already accomplished that), but about choosing to resist the pull of the darkness and walk in the light.

For nearly a decade, I traveled to college campuses as an evangelist sharing the gospel with women. I deeply connected with them because I could relate to the futile search for love in hookups and hangovers that embodies the college party scene. Whenever I speak to an audience such as that, or any group of women who may not know Jesus, I like to tell my personal redemption story; but more important, I love to share God's heart for each woman listening. I believe women who do not know Jesus have a misconception about Him. The enemy has convinced many that God is condemning and could never love them because of their sin. (Let's never forget that Jesus called the enemy the father of lies.) For this reason, I long to teach all women about God's goodness and grace—the same grace that rescued me! I always aim to point women to the cross, where Jesus died to pay for our sins—past, present, and future—and testify that there is no sin beyond His forgiveness.

One of my favorite Bible stories to share is a dramatic scene from Jesus' life found in John 8. In this story, Jesus is confronted by religious leaders with a woman caught in the act of adultery. Now, keep in mind, she has broken God's holy law; and in that day, she could have been stoned to death for such an act. The apostle John, who was as an eyewitness to this event, explains that the religious leaders were using this woman as a pawn to trap Jesus.

Read John 8:1-11. How do you think the woman felt as she was dragged before Jesus in the Temple?

What did Jesus do when the religious leaders accused the woman? (vv. 6-8)

How did Jesus respond to the woman caught in adultery? (vv. 10-11)

This is an incredible story of God's grace. A condemned woman is granted mercy. Try to imagine the fear she felt and the relief that washed over her when Jesus said, "Neither do I condemn you" (v. 11). This is Jesus at His finest—confounding the religious authorities and bringing hope to the hopeless.

Many would stop the story here. Jesus forgives. Hallelujah, this is gospel truth. But the story doesn't end there, and neither does redemption. There is a right response to God's grace that turns from the darkness that held us captive to follow the Light that guides us home. Jesus ends the conversation by saying, "Neither do I condemn you; go, and from now on sin no more." He called her to flee a life of adultery and find real life by following Him.

Now, let's hear Jesus' next recorded words in the context of this dramatic scene.

Write John 8:12 below:

The Bible juxtaposes darkness and light. Throughout Scripture, these two realms are contrasted to represent life without God and life with Him. To the woman caught in adultery, Jesus characterized her old life as "darkness" and called her to leave it behind to follow Him. This brings us back to our Focal Point. As noted, Ephesians was written to believers who lived in a city filled with pagan idolatry, rampant greed, and sexual perversions (sound familiar?). Ephesus was not only a melting pot of cultures; its practices also would cause Las Vegas to blush. What was normal in Ephesus was abhorrent to God. The Christ-followers who lived in that culture were challenged to live radically different from the world around them. The same is true for you and me.

Before I knew Jesus as my Savior, my life was like an episode of the television show *Sex and the City*. I can't judge the woman caught in adultery because I, too, walked in sexual sin and experienced the brokenness it brings. I don't boast in this; I share this part of my story to tell you that Jesus changes *everything*. When Jesus rescued me, He didn't just forgive me and cleanse me of my sin; He also transformed my thinking about sex. I came to see God's design as a beautiful blessing, and I turned from my old life to embrace God's call to walk in purity. I've never once regretted this decision—God is so good. Walking in His light brought restoration to my soul, freedom from my shame, and blessings beyond measure.

The call to walk in the light and reflect God's glory means we lay aside all forms of darkness. Perhaps that is greed or gossip, or maybe it is anger or cursing; whatever form of darkness tempts you today, it is imperative to remember that you are a child of God, a beacon of light. As Ephesians 5:8-9 remind us, "For once you were full of darkness, but now you have light from the Lord. So live as people of light! For this light within you produces only what is good and right and true" (NLT). Your choice to live as a people of light is how you show to the world that Jesus really is better!

Prayer

In the space below, connect with God using your own words:

DAY 3: BE FILLED WITH THE SPIRIT

Focal Point

Begin today's study by reading Ephesians 5:15-20.

The Super Bowl is, hands down, the most hyped sporting event of the year. I'll be honest; I can't remember the last time I watched a single play of the game. Mostly, I go to the parties to hang out with friends and eat yummy foods that require a toothpick. However, the one thing I do watch quite religiously are the commercials. I love the quirky ones, the funny ones, and of course, the heartwarming ones. I'm just saying, anything with a horse gets me crying every single time.

Many years ago, FedEx produced one of my all-time favorite commercials. It was a spoof of the movie *Castaway* starring Tom Hanks. If you haven't seen the film, Hanks plays a FedEx employee stranded on a deserted island. Ultimately, he was rescued and returned home after many years. FedEx produced a brilliant parody of *Castaway* depicting a disheveled employee who returns home with an unopened box he guarded while lost at sea. The faithful employee tracks down the address, rings the doorbell, and presents the customer with her package that was meant to arrive years ago. As he hands over the box, he asks the woman a curious question: "By the way, what's in the package?" The woman opens the box and says, "Nothing really . . . just a satellite phone, GPS locator, fishing rod, water purifier, and some seeds." The commercial closes with the man's look of utter disbelief and regret of what might have been.[3]

Here's the irony: absolutely everything the man needed for survival was with him the entire time he was marooned on that island. All of the depression, starvation, and dehydration could have been avoided had he only opened the box and used the resources in his possession.

I love this commercial because it powerfully illustrates the spiritual truth we are studying today. As God's children, we are indwelled by the Holy Spirit. We've studied aspects of this fact over the past few weeks. However, being *indwelled* by the Spirit of God is different from being *filled* by the Holy Spirit—which is necessary for us to operate or live in the Spirit. We are given God's power to overcome sin, love others, walk in the light, resist temptation, operate in our spiritual gifts, and glorify Jesus. All of these things are in our possession because of the Holy Spirit, but the question remains—have we opened the box?

Filled with the Spirit

Today's Focal Point is a command, or an imperative, that illustrates a spiritual reality. Let's dig into the passage and "open the box," so to speak, to discover the power we possess to live the abundant Christian life.

Review Ephesians 5:15-20 and answer the following:
How are we called to live in verse 15?

What command is given in verse 18?

What happens to a person's thinking, responses, and impulses when "under the influence"? How does a drunk person behave?

Ephesians 5:18 (NIV) says, "Do not get drunk on wine, which leads to debauchery. Instead, be filled with the Spirit." At first glance, this seems to be a command against drunkenness. While we know the Bible discourages such behavior, this passage is using the state of intoxication to illustrate what it means to be "filled with the Spirit."

For starters, the word *drunk* in English means to be intoxicated, which is defined as being "affected by alcohol or drugs especially to the point where physical and mental control is markedly diminished."[4] The one who drinks enough alcohol to reach the state of drunkenness has saturated his or her system to the point that he or she is governed by whatever fills him or her. As a result, the way that one thinks, feels, speaks, reacts, walks, and drives are "under the influence" of the substance. Essentially, a drunk person has handed over control of his or her mind, body, and will to alcohol.

Whatever fills you, controls you.

Back in my wild party girl days, there was a phrase we used to describe this condition, and it was "wasted." As one commentary notes, "Drunkenness is symbolic of the height of folly, the loss of direction, and the waste of a life without God."[5] It means to be squandered. Debauchery is a wasted life rather than a wise life.

Now, the command against drunkenness serves as an illustration for the call to be "filled with the Spirit." Just as someone is filled with alcohol and therefore controlled by alcohol, so we, as God's children, are commanded to "be filled by the Spirit" so that the control of the Holy Spirit marks our lives.

Whenever I teach this truth to women, I like to make this point—whatever fills you, controls you. Just think about it. The person filled with alcohol is controlled by alcohol. The person filled with anger is controlled by anger. The same proves true for lust, greed, and envy. The good news is that this principle also proves true of Jesus. When His Spirit fills us, our thoughts, words, actions, and reactions are under His control. Or rather, they are "under the influence" of God.

When have you experienced being filled and controlled by something (an emotion, a substance, or a thought)?

An explanation of the word *filled* would be helpful at this point. Imagine you are on a sailboat out at sea. For the boat to do what the vessel was intended to do, one vital thing is required—wind. The ship's sail must "be filled" with the wind for it to move forward. This is what the Bible means when it commands us to "be filled with the Spirit." We are the vessel, and we need the Spirit of God to fill us up so that we are propelled forward by His power and love.

So, how do we do this? Think back to the drunkenness illustration. The one who is drunk surrendered control or was "under the

The Big Picture

"Being filled with the Spirit is simply this—having my whole nature yielded to His power. When the whole soul is yielded to the Holy Spirit, God Himself will fill it."

ANDREW MURRAY,
ABSOLUTE SURRENDER[6]

influence." The same holds for the command to be filled by the Spirit. We must daily, and often moment by moment, choose to surrender to the control of the Spirit. This act of surrender says to God, "Your will be done." This yielding releases control of every aspect of our lives to the influence of the Holy Spirit. And as we do, we are propelled by God just as a ship is carried along by the wind at sea.

Yielding Control

The word *yield* means to allow the other to have preference. When I'm driving a car and I see a yield sign, this means I give other cars the right of way. As a Christian, we either yield to our flesh (the old sinful nature) or we yield to the Holy Spirit, who lives within us.

We learned in Ephesians 1:13-14 that at the moment of our salvation, we are sealed with the Spirit. As you recall, this means the Spirit is the One who indwells us, guarantees our redemption, and marks us as God's children. Now that we belong to Christ, our lives give evidence to this new birth or transformed status when we are filled with the Spirit.

When we yield to the Holy Spirit, we are under His control. The more we surrender and give God's will preference in our hearts, the more God produces Christ's character in us. Here's the thing about the Holy Spirit: He is a gentleman. He will not push us or overpower us. We cannot experience His power without totally yielding to Him.

Yielding control to the Holy Spirit requires reminding our flesh (the old sinful nature) who is the boss. The flesh likes to be in control; frankly, it likes to pretend it is God. Unfortunately, when the flesh is in control, the Holy Spirit is not. To yield control to the Spirit means we resist the flesh and obey God's voice however He leads. The more we walk in obedience and yield control to the Holy Spirit, the more we are "under the influence" in every aspect of our lives.

To be filled with the Spirit implies giving Him access to every part of our lives. Imagine handing the key to your spiritual house over to the Lord and telling him to make Himself at home. This is yielding control. When we do this, then the Spirit's power can be exerted through us so that what we do is fruitful for God. It's important to realize that the filling of the Spirit does not apply to outward acts alone; it also applies to the innermost thoughts and motives of our hearts.

Imagine your heart is a literal home to the Holy Spirit. Close your eyes and walk through the house. As you imagine each room, think about what each one represents to you. (For example, the living room could represent your family or entertainment.)

Is there a room where you still need to grant God full access?

Now, invite the Holy Spirit into this area and yield full control to God.

Evidence of a Spirit-Filled Life

What is the evidence or proof that we are Spirit-filled? Notice what Jesus said: "The good man out of the good treasure of his heart brings forth what is good; and the evil *man* out of the evil *treasure* brings forth what is evil; for his mouth speaks from that which fills his heart" (Luke 6:45 NASB). Jesus taught that whatever fills our hearts will fill our mouths.

If we are filled with the Holy Spirit, the proof pours forth in praise. Our Focal Point describes a Spirit-filled person as speaking in psalms, singing hymns, and giving thanks in all things. In my own life, I can easily tell if I'm filled with the Spirit or not. My attitude and words are greatly altered when I'm under the influence of the Spirit. When I'm not, I tend to complain and criticize about petty things. But when the Spirit is controlling me, my heart overflows with praise. Instead of focusing on the negative, I find that I'm grateful and rejoicing in God's blessings.

How about you? What is the evidence that you are filled with the Spirit? What aspect of your character changes when He is in control?

[18]Be filled with the Holy Spirit, [19]singing psalms and hymns and spiritual songs among yourselves, and making music to the Lord in your hearts. [20]And give thanks for everything to God the Father in the name of our Lord Jesus Christ.

EPHESIANS 5:18B-20 NLT

If we are filled with the Holy Spirit, the proof pours forth in praise.

Today we've learned a powerful truth: *whatever fills you, controls you.* As God's masterpiece, who displays His glory to the world, it is paramount that we apprehend the power of God's Spirit to live out the Christian life. God never intended for us to strive for perfection or live in defeat. And that's good news, isn't it? He gave us the Holy Spirit to empower, equip, and fill us. As we surrender to His control, the evidence of the Spirit-filled life manifests in our lives. Just as wind fills the sails of a ship and propels it forward, we are propelled by God's Spirit to live for His glory. Let's surrender and be filled!

Prayer

In the space below, connect with God using your own words:

DAY 4: MARRIAGE, FOR HIS GLORY

Focal Point

Begin today's study by reading Ephesians 5:21-33.

Confession time. I put the "pro" in procrastination this week. I did my absolute best to postpone writing today's lesson. I rearranged my daughter's bedroom, thoroughly cleaned my office, and scrolled through social media longer than I care to admit. Why? Because I was flat-out intimidated by the topic of marriage.

Our Focal Point, Ephesians 5:21-33, is considered by theologians as the most important teaching on marriage in the entire Bible. (No pressure!) Besides, having been married for only seven short years, I thought, "Who am I to advise anyone about this weighty topic?" Oh, and another intimidating factor—I'm writing to twenty-first-century women, and I get the fun task of throwing around words like *submission* and *headship*. (Good golly, Miss Molly; I'd rather clean my toilets!)

I'm joking about the toilets of course, but I do tread lightly into today's teaching recognizing that we are all in a wide variety of life stages. Some of you are married, while others are single, divorced, or even widowed. Some marriages are thriving, while others are in trauma. So, as we explore what the Bible says about marriage, I realize that even reading the words can evoke pain in some and longing in others. Therefore, as your sister in Christ and someone who lived for many years desiring to be married, I proceed with sensitivity.

For all of these reasons, I finally stopped procrastinating and prayed. I asked the Lord for a word, and I sensed Him say, "Do not fear this topic! Marriage, as I intended it, is for your good and for my glory!"

For His Glory. I thought about those three words and how often we've read them in Ephesians. After all, our redemption is "for His glory" and marriage (as we will see) mirrors our relationship with Christ. While God's purpose in marriage is good, the reality is that darkness hates the light and marriage is under attack.

Friend, we live in a broken world that has desecrated marriage. Just because sinful humans have fractured the institution, that doesn't mean God's beautiful design was wrong or doesn't work. The Lord desires for us to know that His purpose for marriage is to bless us. When redeemed men and women live according to God's design, then marriage showcases His glory to the world. Marriage conducted God's way is a magnificent demonstration of the grace that unites us with Christ. So, whether you are married or single, I believe there is a word for each of us today as we discover how God designed marriage to display His lavish love to the world.

Let's proceed into today's study trusting in God's goodness and with eyes ready to behold His glorious design for marriage.

Reading a portion of Scripture out of context is dangerous. Before examining our Focal Point, let's begin by reading **all** *of Ephesians 5 and then answering the following questions:*

The Big Picture

"The doctrine of the Trinity, which Jesus endorsed and Scripture teaches, also profoundly affects Christian marriage. The Father, Son, and Holy Spirit live in a permanent, plural, equal, complementary, ordered, and loving union. And since we're created like God, we thrive in marriage relationships that mirror his trinitarian union."[7]

Ephesians 5:1 sets the stage for our discussion of marriage. What are we (God's children) called to do?

According to verse 8, how are we called to walk?

Now, how does verse 15 encourage us to walk?

With what are we to "be filled"? (v. 18)

As children of God, we are called to live radically different from the world. The words *light* and *darkness* contrast this difference. Reviewing Ephesians 5, we see Christians are called to walk worthy of our calling as God's masterpiece by imitating Jesus' love, walking in His light, and being filled with His Spirit. This calling powerfully sets the stage for the biblical definition of marriage, which is to showcase Christ's love for the church.

Let's have a little fun. Reread Ephesians 5:21-33 and complete the following exercise:

Each time you see the word **wife***, mark it with a diamond, and mark the word* **husband** *with a cross. Example:*

"Husbands love your wife as Christ loved the church."

Now read the verses again, and this time mark the words **submit** *with a circle* ● *and* **love** *with a heart* ♥*.*

What does verse 21 call both husbands and wives to do?

What do verses 22-24 call wives to do? Why?

According to verses 25-29, what are husbands to do?

*Verse 31 gives us the biblical definition for marriage by saying,
"the _____ become _____ flesh."*

*Paul says this "one flesh" union is a profound mystery. What
does this mystery represent? (v. 32)*

*What final commands are given to the husband and wife in
verse 33?*

As we dive into this Scripture, it can raise a host of questions
pertaining to the roles within marriage. The primary question
revolves around the word *submission*. As modern women, we
can bristle when we hear this word, and rightly so because it has
been greatly abused in the past—which is why it is imperative
that we read the entire verse in context. Those who have abused
this word obviously have failed to read the call to husbands to
sacrificially love their wives as Christ loves the church, as God's
Word so clearly states in Ephesians 5:25.

Today committed Christ-followers hold various opinions
on roles within marriage. The two primary camps are
complementarianism and egalitarianism, which are "theological
views on the relationship between men and women, especially
in marriage and in ministry. Complementarianism stresses that
although men and women are equal in personhood, they are
created for different roles. Egalitarianism also agrees that men and
women are equal in personhood but holds that there are no gender-
based limitations on the roles of men and women."[8]

It is my personal belief that there is room at God's table for those who differ on this topic. The important point on which we all can agree is found in Ephesians 5:21, which talks of "submitting to one another out of reverence for Christ" (ESV). In other words, regardless of the view one holds, biblical submission within marriage occurs when a couple's hearts are surrendered to God and they allow Him to lead their home, being subject to one another out of reverence for Christ.

I have good Christian friends who are egalitarians, sharing leadership in the home. Personally, I hold a complementarian view of marriage, which means I believe that men and women are equal in status and personhood but have different roles in the relationship. I base this upon the model we see in the Trinity, where each person of the Godhead (Father, Son, and Holy Spirit) is equal in status and personhood but holds different roles or functions. Therefore, just as Jesus submitted to the Father, so I choose to submit to my husband. This simply means I allow my husband the space to steer our family. I affirm his role as head of the home because I believe that, as the spiritual leader, he bears the burden of responsibility before God to lead and protect his family—being accountable before the Lord for how he loves and leads his family. I see my role as encouraging and equipping him for that responsibility.

Having said that, please note that I do *not* believe submission is a license for husbands to do what they want to do. Because many have twisted the word and its meaning to the detriment of women, it's important to clarify what submission is *not*:

> **Submission does not mean the dominance of the man.** A wife is not a servant in her home meant to tend to her husband's wishes or to acquiesce to every decision. In just a few verses after Paul's instruction to wives, he tells the husband to lay down his life for his wife and love her "as Christ loved the church" (verse 25). A husband who loves his wife in this way is not a tyrant, a demanding brute, or a demeaning bully but a compassionate, considerate, and encouraging champion or advocate.

Submission does not mean abusive relationships.
Many bristle at the word because it has been horrifically misused. As one pastor warns, "This means that if your husband tells you to do something that would make you disobey the Lord or . . . ever puts you or your family in harm's way, you need to get out of there, and you need to get some counseling to help you heal."[9]

Submission does not mean to all men. The text doesn't mean that all women everywhere should submit to all men, as if women cannot be leaders. We need the leadership of women in our world today, offering their gifts and wisdom in the workplace, government, community, and church.

Again, submission is never license for husbands to do what they want to do. Rather, it is empowerment to do what they ought to do, which is to love their wives as Christ loves the church. Speaking of a man's role, let's look closer at the high calling God's word gives to the husband in marriage.

Called to Cherish

Cherish is one of my all-time favorite words. It isn't overused as its sister synonym *love* is. I like to think of *cherish* as love wearing work boots. The call to cherish stands in vivid contrast to a world where women are treated as commodities or mere sexual objects. Without exaggeration, the biblical definition of marriage and the duties given to husbands to love their wives as Christ loved the church literally changed the world.

Keep in mind, women didn't have political power during the Roman era. Women were under the authority of men. Even Jewish women couldn't testify in court, pray in public, or learn to read. Additionally, the husband's duty outlined in these verses was so different from the Roman concepts of marriage that the first-century readers would have been shocked. Paul's words massively elevated the status of women in the culture of the time it was written.

[28]So husbands ought also to love their own wives as their own bodies. He who loves his own wife loves himself; [29]for no one ever hated his own flesh, but nourishes and cherishes it, just as Christ also *does* the church, [30]because we are members of His body.
EPHESIANS 5:28-30 NASB

In verse 25, Paul begins to address the husband's duties in marriage. At that time, it was popularly acknowledged that wives had obligations to their husbands, but not vice versa. Men virtually had free will to do anything and to divorce at whim. The command for husbands to cherish their wives was a radically new concept.

How is the husband called to love? As Christ loved the church. Jesus modeled love by sacrificing Himself to redeem His bride. Husbands are commanded by God to model this same sacrificial care for their wives. One commentary notes, "(1) He should be willing to sacrifice everything for her. (2) He should make her well-being of primary importance. (3) He should care for her as he cares for his own body. No wife needs to fear submitting to a man who treats her in this way."[10] To this I say, "Amen!"

God reveals His covenantal love through the union between a husband and wife. As a husband and wife practice their God-given roles of sacrificial love and honoring, the gospel is portrayed. Just as we become one with Christ at our salvation, so husband and wife become one flesh in marriage. This spiritual mystery is profound indeed, and the means by which God showcases the gospel.

Submission in Real Life

My husband and I said "I do" outside my family's barn in East Texas amid horses, longhorn steer, and a miniature donkey. While *Pinterest* may have prepared me for planning a gorgeous rustic wedding, nothing prepared this independent single woman for submission in marriage. Regardless if you are a complementarian or egalitarian, the call to surrender your will to the will of another is not easy. I was thirty-eight years old when we came together as husband and wife. I was far older than most women who marry for the first time, and I'd been living on my own for twenty years. Aside from the independence factor, I'm also what people kindly call "strong-willed." I wasn't blind to these challenges, but I was also madly in love and extremely optimistic. The call to "Submit to one another out of reverence for Christ" seemed like a wonderful idea . . . on paper. Living this command out in my daily life would prove to be an opportunity for growth!

Real life offers plenty of opportunities for differing opinions and conflicting agendas in a home. After all, I'd lived on my own, paid my own bills, and traveled the world long before I met him. So, the choice to submit was one I made out of obedience to the Lord.

Over the past few years, when my husband and I came head-to-head over an issue, my flesh naturally wanted to fight for dominance. The times when I indulged my flesh and fought for control, I could feel a seismic shift in our home; the alignment was off. Choosing my way and being unwilling to listen to his opinions or ideas caused major conflict. I can also testify that when I've submitted (even when it's hard), I've seen God move powerfully in our marriage, and I've watched my husband take responsibility in ways that bring peace and stability to our home.

There is order within the Godhead, and this order is mirrored in marriage. Jesus, the Son, is equal in divinity and power with God the Father and the Holy Spirit. While they are equal, there is mutual submission within the persons of the Trinity. Marriage beautifully models this triune relationship.

Friend, I love how God's word is applicable to every facet of our lives. After all, we are called to live as God's masterpiece in the real world, where we showcase His glory in the midst of real relationships and real struggles. Many of you walking through this study of Ephesians are single; others of you are married. Regardless of your relationship status, it proves vital in a world filled with mixed messages about marriage for us to look to God's Word in this time of conflicting voices. Wherever we might land regarding the roles of husbands and wives, Paul sets forth marriage as one of the ways that we "imitate" God's sacrificial love and show the world the kind of love that willingly lays its life down for the good of another. It is this divine love that marriage is meant to reveal and we can only manifest when we are filled with God's Spirit. It is my prayer that God's lavish love fills you up today and overflows to those He places before you.

Prayer

In the space below, connect with God using your own words:

DAY 5: HONOR YOUR PARENTS

Focal Point

Begin today's study by reading Ephesians 6:1-9.

My hometown boasts some incredible hiking trails. A nearby path winds through rugged Texas terrain and rewards hikers with a panoramic view of our city. A few weeks ago, I hiked this trail with a friend, and we got lost. We circled a few times before realizing we were off course. In the thick trees and jagged boulders, everything began to look the same. Finally, we found a map with the three best words any lost hiker can ever read: "YOU ARE HERE." Stopping to get our bearings helped us navigate our way back to the main trail and head for home.

As we've journeyed through Ephesians, it is easy for us to get a little lost. From day to day, the topics have changed; and if we aren't careful, it's easy to feel like they aren't cohesive. But this is far from the truth. There is one driving point to this epistle, and it is vital to know so that we don't get off track: **We are God's masterpiece, redeemed to live for His glory.** We must come back to this point so we can know where we are going.

I want to begin today's study by stating, "YOU ARE HERE." Remember, Ephesians can be summarized in three words—sit, walk, stand. Let's look at each one briefly.

Sit. The first section, chapters 1–2, focuses on our position; we are *seated* with Christ in the heavenly realms. "Seated with Christ" means we are united with Him in His victory over sin and death.

Jesus' victory is our victory.

Jesus' righteousness is our righteousness.

Jesus' life is our life.

We learned that Jesus accomplished our redemption with His blood and the Holy Spirit sealed the finished work. Now, because of this redemption, we are beloved children of God, and this is a gift of grace. As a result, we can rest in our new identity just as one would cease working and sit in a chair.

Walk. The second section of Ephesians focuses on our walk, which refers to how we live our daily lives. In chapters 3, 4, and 5 we are called to "walk worthy" of our calling as God's masterpiece, which is our response to God's grace. So far, we've learned to walk in love, walk in the light, and walk in the power of the Holy Spirit.

Stand. Next week we will shift the focus of our study to the word *stand* and discover how we can resist the spiritual forces of darkness that oppose us as God's masterpiece.

Before we do that, we have one final lesson today about how we walk. Since our calling is to showcase God's glory to the world, one major arena in which we manifest His character is our family relationships. While we could spend ample time on each family relationship, we will target the one that we all experience—honoring parents (or caregivers). Each of us is someone's child (or dependent), and our responses to them impact us immensely.

Review Ephesians 6:1-9 and answer the following questions:
Why are children commanded to obey their parents? (v. 1)

In verse 2, we are commanded to honor our father and mother.
What motivation is given in verse 3 for honoring them?

Pause to reflect on your relationship with your parents or
whoever raised you. Do you feel you honor them as Scripture
commands? Why or why not?

It is important to clarify that *obeying* and *honoring* are different. One commentary notes, "To obey means to do what another says to do; to honor means to respect and love. Children are to obey while under their parents' care, but they must honor their parents for life."[11] Verse 3 adds the motivation for honoring our parents: "that it may go well with you" (v. 3). This New Testament promise is founded upon Old Testament principles (Exodus 20:12 and Deuteronomy 5:16).

Our God is a God of order. He positioned the family as the fabric of society. He placed parents as the authority over their children. Within this framework, a child learns to respect authority and ultimately to honor God. Natural consequences arise when this authority structure is broken. Children who disrespect parents become adults who disrespect authority and do not fear the Lord. The fifth commandment is central to God's law and includes promises of blessings for those who obey it. But putting it into practice in the real world can be complicated. Legitimate questions arise, such as

How do I honor an abusive parent?

How do I honor a parent with whom I'm estranged or who walked out?

How do I respect a parent whose behavior isn't respectable?

These questions are valid; and let's face it, even as adults, our relationships with our parents can be messy. Where do we begin?

Jesus said the whole law is summed up in one word: *love.* Loving God and loving others is the evidence that we are God's masterpiece. Obedience to His commands is our response to His lavish grace. We are called to extend to others the same mercy given to us—and this includes our parents.

I had been walking with Jesus for about five years when the Lord began a profound work of healing in my heart. This work exposed childhood wounds that had festered into bitterness. While I could see the evidence of my new life in Christ when with my friends and church family, I struggled to "walk worthy" whenever I went home to visit my family. Something was terribly wrong. Although I was redeemed, I didn't produce the fruit of the Spirit (love, joy, peace, patience, or kindness); instead, I exhibited anger, impatience, and resentment. This bad fruit led me to discover the bad root—bitterness.

This bitterness traced back to the trauma I had experienced when I was sexually abused as a little girl. While I've already shared briefly of this abuse, sharing my response to it is crucial as we look together at the command to honor our parents.

Friend, the Lord loves us too much to let us remain unhealed, so He led me through a season of inner healing. What I mean by "inner healing" is that I began to deal with my painful past by acknowledging the damage done and forgiving the offenders. In this process, I came to see how I had coped with my abuse in sinful ways.

I needed to repent of dishonoring my father and mother. As a little girl, my parents were ignorant of the abuse. I didn't have the capacity at that young age to see that they were innocent. So, I projected my pain onto them and hated them for something that they didn't do. I assumed they didn't love me (because they failed to protect me), so I tried to push them out of my life. As a result, this projection led to my sins of unforgiveness, rebellion, judgmental attitudes, and disrespect.

I share this story because I did not honor my parents for years. I spoke harshly to them. I criticized them. My patience was short and my temper quick. I did not walk in a manner worthy of Christ. The Holy Spirit convicted me of my sin but also showed me how my rebellion was hindering me from experiencing God's best. After all, the command to honor our parents includes a promise for those who obey.

As I recognized my sin, I repented. I genuinely grieved how I had disobeyed God's command to honor them. I also invited the Lord to heal the wounded places where the bitterness resided. Through this process, I forgave my parents for their mistakes and the ways they had unknowingly failed me. One of the reasons I call myself a Redeemed Girl is because Jesus has redeemed lost years. He has restored my relationship with my parents, and now I have a deep respect for both of them and treasure our relationship. Only God could have done this work!

Why do I tell you this? God's command to honor our parents is for our good. You may have wonderful parents who loved you well; praise God for that. Or you may have been deeply wounded by one or both, and the Lord invites you to forgive them and find healing. Wherever you are on the spectrum, I want to challenge all of us to put this command into practice. I can testify to God's faithfulness. As I repented and began to honor my parents, the Lord has showered my life with the most incredible blessings.

What are some practical ways we can honor our parents? For starters, we can't wait for them to be worthy; we must choose to obey

God's command to honor our parents is for our good.

the Lord regardless of how they act. I once heard a teacher explain it to me this way: *when we can't honor the person, we honor the position.* Here are two ways we can put this commandment into practice.

1. Forgive Them

As we think of the ways our parents hurt or disappointed us, I want to acknowledge that some of you endured great trauma at the hands of those who were supposed to be your primary source of love and nurture. Forgiveness, especially toward parents, is not a quick process. But the first step in honoring them is acknowledging that they are broken, sinful people just as we are. As God's redeemed, we are to offer the same grace that has been given to us. Forgiveness doesn't mean that we dismiss sinful behavior or erase the past, but it does mean that we release the person to God, who is the ultimate judge. Through forgiveness we imagine our parent(s) standing at the foot of the cross next to us and we offer them the same mercy that Jesus extends to us. (Please note: It is important in cases of abuse to seek professional help from a Christian counselor who can help you walk through the trauma you've experienced.)

Read Jesus' words in Matthew 18:21-35 about forgiveness. How many times did Jesus tell Peter to forgive? (v. 22)

Jesus told Peter a story to illustrate why we should forgive. What does Jesus teach us about forgiveness through this story? (vv. 23-35)

Pause and think about your mom and dad (or caregivers). Do you need to forgive them for anything? Don't rush this process.

Ask the Holy Spirit to reveal any bitterness in your heart and then write a prayer of forgiveness below, specifically naming the offense(s) and releasing each person to the Lord. (Keep in mind, this is an ongoing process. Allow the Lord to show you what needs to be released today.)

2. Speak Well of Them

Words are powerful. I've come to realize that it is just as simple to speak about someone's good qualities as it is their negative ones—though it's not always easy. When we choose to speak well of our parents (or caregivers), we honor them. The opposite also proves true: when our words become bitter, our minds tend to focus on the negative; and we continually spew toxic speech. Choosing to speak well is an act of obedience to the Lord and ultimately keeps our hearts from bitterness. James 3:5 (NASB) says, "The tongue is a small part of the body, and yet it boasts of great things. See how great a forest is set aflame by such a small fire!" Words can bring death or life. Choose to use words about your parent(s) that will bring life. Here are a few ways to speak life:

> *Think of positive attributes your parent(s) passed on to you and speak of these things.*

> *Consider the sacrifices your parent(s) made for you and praise them for these things.*

> *Recognize the hardships your parent(s) overcame and honor them for this.*

If you struggle to think of anything good, such as in the case of an abusive or absent parent, acknowledge the sin to God and extend grace to the sinner by praying for him or her. And again, if you're not yet ready to extend grace, ask God to help you get there. Even that simple prayer is a first step toward honoring your parents.

As God's masterpiece, we are called to walk worthy of Him, which means we exhibit His goodness and grace for the world to see.

Let's practice this together. List three positive attributes or characteristics your parent(s) passed on to you. (Or if you're unable to do this, write a prayer below asking for God's help in honoring your parents.)

As God's masterpiece, we are called to walk worthy of Him, which means we exhibit His goodness and grace for the world to see. Friend, as we honor our parents, we honor God. We show Jesus that we love Him through our obedience, and we show our parents the grace that He has given us. Who knows? Perhaps an unbelieving parent will see the glory of Christ and turn to Him in repentance. Perhaps through your obedience, a rift in the family could be healed. It's amazing how one act of obedience can transform someone's destiny. I'm praying for you today that your heart would be healed of wounds and bitterness and filled up with God's love that can overflow to others, especially your parents. To God be the glory!

Prayer

In the space below, connect with God using your own words:

SESSION 6: VIDEO VIEWER GUIDE

Ephesians 6:10-13 – Armor of God

Be _____ in the Lord.

Ephesians 1:18-21 – Jesus won, the enemy is defeated
2 Chronicles 20:12 – Strong in the Lord
2 Chronicles 20:15 – The battle is God's

Put on the full _____ of God.

_____ _____ .

> What does it mean to stand?
> We choose to believe God.
> We choose to let God fight our battles.
> We choose not to look at the natural but at what God can do in the supernatural.

Ephesians 3:14-21 – Prayer of blessing: be filled with the fullness of God

WEEK 6: VICTORIOUS SAINTS

Overview

In Ephesians we learn about our victorious position in Christ as children of God. The first half of the epistle focuses on the realities of our salvation and what Christ accomplished for us on the cross. We are God's masterpiece; this is both our identity and our calling. The second half teaches us how to walk and showcase His glory to the world. In the final chapter, we are taught to "stand firm" in our victorious position and not give sway to the schemes of the enemy. This week we learn the various pieces of the spiritual armor granted to us in Christ and how we resist the spiritual forces of darkness that oppose us. This final week is filled with practical tools to help us resist the enemy and stand as God's masterpiece.

DAY 1: STAND YOUR GROUND

Focal Point

Begin today's study by reading Ephesians 6:10-13.

Huddled together with my husband and bonus-boys while on safari in South Africa, we watched as a young lion, the king of the jungle, stalked its prey in the wild. The sun had set, so we observed nature from beneath a bright moon and our guide's steady flashlight. With breathless anticipation, we sat silently and motionless as the ferocious cat used deathly precision to capture its victim. All that stood between us and the lion was an open-air, topless Land Cruiser. At any moment that lion could have redirected its gaze, and we would have been kitty litter.

Wildlife experts teach that the best response to a lion attack is to stand firm and hold your ground. The *Smithsonian* writes: "The first thing to know about surviving a lion attack is to not run. It should not surprise you that a lion is way faster than you, but in case you need numbers: the fastest human to ever live, Usain Bolt, can run 27.79 miles per hour. A lion can run 50 miles per hour. So stand still. If you run, you'll only die tired."[1]

Scripture warns, "Be alert and of sober mind. Your enemy the devil prowls around like a roaring lion looking for someone to devour" (1 Peter 5:8 NIV). Today we will discover in Ephesians 6 that, as with a lion in Africa, our best strategy against the devil's schemes is to stand our ground.

Stand Against the Devil's Schemes

Today's Focal Point gives us an explicit instruction: *stand*. We will soon explore what this word means, but first, let's examine more closely why we are called to stand. In Ephesians 6:10-13, the apostle Paul shifts his focus from how a Christ-follower should live in this world to the call to stand against the spiritual forces that oppose us. As we see in 1 Peter 5:8, the apostle Peter warns us of a similar reality, telling us that the devil is like a roaring lion seeking someone to devour. Who is this lion or enemy that the Bible warns of?

In Week 1 of our study, we briefly touched on the fact that we have an enemy. Jesus told us that our enemy's agenda is to "steal and kill and destroy" (John 10:10). We compared this to Hitler's ambition during World War II to amass the world's great masterpieces for himself. Our enemy, who goes by many names in Scripture, seeks to destroy God's masterpiece (you and me) and thwart our divine purpose, which is to manifest God's glory to the world. With this background in mind, we turn our attention to the final section of Ephesians, which addresses the spiritual war that all believers face.

Refer again to Ephesians 6:10-13 (NIV) and answer the questions below and on the next page:

What is the first word of the passage? _____

With the word *finally* in Ephesians 6:10, the apostle Paul connects this closing section of Ephesians with all that was previously stated concerning our position in Christ. One commentator makes this observation:

> In light of all that God has done for you.
> In light of the glorious standing you have
> as a child of God.
> In light of His great plan of the ages that
> God has made you part of.
> In light of the plan for Christian maturity
> and growth He gives to you.
> In light of the conduct God calls every
> believer to live.
> In light of the filling of the Spirit and our
> walk in the Spirit.
> In light of all this, there is a battle to
> fight in the Christian life.[2]

What specific instruction does Paul give in verse 10?

What are we called to "put on"? (v. 11)

Why are we instructed to put on this armor?
"That you may be able to _____ *." (v. 11)*

Verse 12 clarifies that our struggle or battle is not
against _____ *.*

What four things do we battle against? (v. 12)

> *We don't fight **for** victory but **from** a place of victory.*

Now, let's notice a few key points from this passage. First, we are called to be "strong" in Jesus' mighty power. As Christ-followers, we don't have to be victims of the enemy's schemes; we are equipped to stand. Jesus' mighty power is within us, and the Word of God declares that "the one who is in you is greater than the one who is in the world" (1 John 4:4 NIV). We must understand it is only in the name of Jesus and His power that we can stand against the evil that oppresses us.

Next, notice the text does not say *if* the day of evil comes but *when* the day of evil comes. Spiritual warfare is a reality all believers will face. Therefore, if we are to experience victory in this life, we must learn to stand. It is not only missionaries or some elite group of Christians who experience warfare. The Bible is clear about this. While I don't want us to become women who are hyper-focused on the darkness, I believe that one of Satan's chief strategies for our destruction is our denial of his existence. And, in fact, some Christians doubt or deny the reality of his existence. Pastor Steven J. Cole writes:

> It is vital for your survival as a Christian that you realize that when you became a Christian, you were drafted into God's army. Daily you are engaged in a battle with an unseen spiritual enemy that seeks to destroy you. Otherwise, when trials hit, you will think that something is wrong. You will wonder why God has allowed this. You won't understand the reality of your situation.[3]

Let's be crystal clear: Jesus is victorious. One thing we have celebrated in our study of Ephesians is the fact that through Christ's death and resurrection, He shattered the enemy's hold on us. Jesus "delivered us from the domain of darkness and transferred us to the kingdom of his beloved Son" (Colossians 1:13). We are now seated victoriously with Christ. We don't fight *for* victory but *from* a place of victory. Knowing the difference is a game changer.

This good news is rooted in the gospel, but just because we are no longer slaves to the darkness does not mean that the enemy stops harassing us as children of God. The New Testament repeatedly attests to the fact that a spiritual battle rages, and we must know how to stand our ground if we are to overcome. That is why Ephesians 6:11 (NIV) calls us to "put on the full armor of God" so that we can stand against the "devil's schemes."

What does the word **scheme** *bring to mind? Have you ever fallen victim to a scheme?*

A few years ago, my family hosted a young woman who was immigrating to the United States. As she was new to our country, she was not familiar with our rules and customs. One afternoon she ran into my kitchen telling me that the police were coming to arrest her. I couldn't fathom why, and she was crying hysterically. I knew that she hadn't done anything illegal. So, after getting her to calm down and explain the full story to me, I quickly realized she was victim of a phone scam that convinced her that she owed "the government" thousands of dollars. The scheme to steal money from my friend worked. Although she didn't owe any money, she believed the liar on the other end of the phone and was sending cash because she feared she would be arrested otherwise. This is a perfect illustration of what Scripture means when it says "the devil's schemes."

While the New Testament warns of this ongoing battle against the enemy, many Christians are blind to Satan's devices. I know I have been blind to them myself far too many times. While all of our struggles can't be blamed on schemes of the enemy, each of us has our own fleshly desires that lead us astray and we live in a broken world; but Scripture does expose the reality of spiritual warfare. Often we assume the attacks that knock us down time and time again are just our own thoughts, fears, weaknesses, and emotions. If we are to stand firm in this day, we must open our eyes to the various assaults that seek to topple us. Concerning the schemes of the Enemy, Chip Ingram writes this:

> [Satan's schemes] are orchestrated in order to tempt us, deceive us, draw us away from God, fill our hearts with half-truths and untruths, and lure us into pursuing good things in the wrong way, at the wrong time, or with the wrong person. The English word *strategies* is derived from the Greek word Paul uses that is translated "schemes." That means our temptations are not random. The false perspectives we encounter do not come at us haphazardly. The lies we hear, the conflicts we have with others, the cravings that consume us when we are at our weakest points—they are all part of a plan to make us casualties in the invisible war. They are organized, below-the-belt assaults designed to neutralize the very people God has filled with his awesome power.[4]

Friends, spiritual warfare comes in many forms and proves unique to each person. I believe the enemy tailors his attacks to suit his target. In my life, attacks usually come when I'm tired, burned out, and preparing for a major ministry event. It is in these moments that my thoughts become prey to condemnation, temptation, or unhealthy suggestions. Here are some of the various schemes I've noticed that the enemy employs to oppose us:

- **Deception**—teachings or philosophies that contradict God's truth.
- **Intimidation**—overt pressure to silence us from being bold in our faith or living for Christ.
- **Distraction**—the daily noise and interruptions that keep us from reading the Bible, praying, or serving God.
- **Temptation**—thoughts that seek to justify sin, undermining the goodness of God and questioning the authority of His Word.

* Seduction—intense pull toward ungodliness that lures us away from God.
* Condemnation—shame and guilt heaped upon us when we fall into sin combined with the thought that forgiveness is not available.
* Accusation—negative suggestions, speculations, and projections about ourselves, others, or God that divide and destroy fellowship in the body of Christ.

As you review the list above, what is one scheme you have personally experienced? Share how this tactic worked in your life to pull you away from Jesus or weakened your ability to glorify Him?

It's one thing to acknowledge that spiritual warfare exists, but how do we know when we are in the midst of it? For the vast majority of us, the battle rages against our minds. For instance, when the serpent went after Eve in the garden of Eden, he didn't use blunt force. He used words, just as the enemy does with us today:

* The enemy uses shame to heap condemnation on our hearts.
* The enemy uses fearful suggestions to cripple us with anxiety.
* The enemy uses accusations to divide marriages, friendships, and family relationships.
* The enemy uses seeds of doubt that lead us to question God and His Word and walk in sin.

My mentor is fond of saying, "The enemy is the enemy." I quote her here because our Focal Point reminds us that our battle is not against "flesh and blood." As we look at a few of the methods the enemy uses to attack us, we see how these schemes easily affect our relationships with others. It's easy to point the finger at our husband or coworker or the other driver in traffic and get angry or resentful. But if we stop and evaluate the situation, we can recognize there is another who is behind the conflict.

Notice how the schemes of the enemy begin in our minds. As you review that list of schemes, take note of how each is first a thought that leads to an action or behavior. Over the next few days, we will learn how to stand and how each piece of the armor of God equips us for victory. I pray today's teaching has equipped you with discernment to recognize the enemy's schemes. Yes, warfare is real; but as we've learned in Ephesians, Jesus wins!

Prayer

In the space below, connect with God using your own words:

DAY 2: THE ARMOR OF GOD, PART 1

Focal Point

Begin today's study by reading Ephesians 6:10-18.

Waves of accusation crashed against my mind: *No one loves you. You are unwanted; you always have been, and you always will be.* This spiritual battle began about three weeks prior to a conference my ministry hosts for women. Every year we experience spiritual warfare leading up to this event. But this summer, the battle for my mind was so sinister that I didn't realize I was under attack until it engulfed me.

As we studied yesterday, our enemy custom-tailors schemes that are designed to hinder each of us from living for God's glory. Today's Focal Point tells us that we can expect these schemes "when the day of evil comes" (Ephesians 6:13 NIV). The "day of evil" is not some distant, future event but anytime that the enemy sets his sights on us, God's masterpiece. In my case, the battle came prior to my biggest ministry event of the year. That summer thoughts of rejection tormented me—immense feelings of being unwanted and unloved that didn't have a basis in reality. My fears seemed so real, especially when random circumstances appeared to validate the taunts. For example, a friend would forget to call me back, or my sweet husband would make a simple remark that I would completely misinterpret. Crazy junk.

No one loves you! My heart was engulfed with the searing pain of rejection. My mind swirled with these dark thoughts. Can I be honest? I'm embarrassed to share this story, but here's what I've come to realize: I'm not alone in this battle. I know our enemy uses similar tactics with each of us.

To say that particular attack came out of the blue is an understatement. At the time, I was blessed with an incredible family, strong friendships, and the sweetest marriage. When the intense feelings of rejection hit, I could not be reasoned with; I felt completely unloved. My whole identity was under attack. (Please note, I said my *identity* was under attack.) Today, I know precisely what Scripture means by "fiery darts."

Satan's fiery darts ripped through me, striking at old wounds of abandonment and rejection from my childhood that were easy targets for his lies. My heart brimmed with a pain that would not relent. If I had been talking with someone else experiencing these types of negative thoughts, I would have recognized it as spiritual warfare and prayed for the individual. But in the midst of it myself, I couldn't discern that my thoughts were lies and not based in truth. That's the thing about the enemy's schemes: we don't easily recognize that we are being deceived, which is why it is so important to talk to a pastor or counselor when struggling with negative thoughts. (We should never walk through this type of battle alone.)

Once the conference started, it felt like the attacks ramped up. At one point, I found myself hidden away crying in a shower because I didn't want anyone else to know. My mind felt like a combat zone. The next night, I experienced a breakthrough that taught me how to stand and put on the armor of God.

During worship, we sang songs of praise. Friend, worship is a great way to turn the battle with the evil one in the right direction. Satan can't stand it when we lift up Jesus' name in praise. As we sang, I could feel the presence of God in our worship. At one point, we sang "Good Good Father." The song's chorus is so simple, but it holds such a profound message about God's goodness and how He loves us as His children. That is our identity. Even though my heart was still in shreds, by faith I declared that God is a good father and that I am loved by Him!

As we worshiped, the darkness lifted. As I like to say, "Worship wins the war." The clouds over my mind dispersed and I could see the Light! Once again, I could sense God's love for me as His beloved daughter. Little did I know it at the time, but I was clothing myself with the armor of God and standing firm against the enemy.

As I sang, I fastened *the belt of truth* and proclaimed that I am a beloved child of God. I secured *the helmet of salvation* and reminded myself that I was chosen before the foundation of the world. I picked up *the shield of faith*, believing in the goodness of my God, and I extinguished the fiery darts of the enemy.

I love this quotation by pastor and author Tim Keller: "What is putting on the armor? To put it on means to take the privileges of the gospel and the benefits of the gospel and begin to use them in your life so as to create a new disposition, a new habitual way of thinking about yourself and all of the people around you."[5] That is precisely what I did that day. I took hold of the truth of the gospel and began to use it as an offensive weapon against the darkness that surrounded me. I allowed the truth of what Jesus accomplished for me to reorient my self-perception and identity: *I am a child of God!*

Read Ephesians 6:10-18 again and answer the following questions:
Why are we instructed to put on the armor of God? (v. 13)

Six pieces of armor are listed in verses 14-18. List each below:

1.

2.

3.

4.

5.

6.

> *There is nothing in the world like worship to break the power of the evil one.*

Let's explore each piece of the armor, focusing on three today and three tomorrow.

Put on the Full Armor of God

To understand the background of the command "put on the full armor of God," we need to remember that the apostle Paul is a prisoner in Rome when writing this letter. Paul is in the custody of Roman soldiers who guard him. It's easy to imagine that he has carefully observed how a soldier's armor fits together and provides protection in battle.

It's also worth noting that Paul knows of spiritual warfare from personal experience. This man has been beaten, tortured, falsely accused, and physically thrown out of cities. The enemy is not happy about Paul's ministry. So when this great man teaches us to "stand firm," we know that he speaks from personal experience; and we are wise to sit up, take note, and listen to what he teaches. This advice is not from a mere spectator; it comes from a sage soldier in God's army giving a report from the front lines of battle. He knows the enemy's schemes personally.

Note that the apostle Paul divides the armor into two main sections. The first set contains the three articles a Christ-follower should wear at all times: the belt of truth, breastplate of righteousness, and shoes of peace. These pieces of armor are our ongoing, daily protection against spiritual warfare. The final three pieces that we'll examine tomorrow—the helmet of salvation, the shield of faith, and the sword of the Spirit—are defensive weapons we "take up" when the battle rages. As we will discover, each piece of our spiritual armor corresponds to truth Paul has taught us in Ephesians. Let's dive into the first three pieces of armor that we wear every day.

The Belt of Truth
When most of us dress, a belt is an afterthought or the last article of clothing we put on. But for the Roman soldier, the belt was essential because it held the entire armor together. This understanding proves imperative for us in our desire to stand firm; without the belt of truth, nothing in our lives holds together.

Look up John 14:6. Who does Jesus say He is?

Read Ephesians 1:13 in the margin. What word is used to describe the gospel in this verse?

The message of _____.

One commentary notes, "To belt on truth means to be strengthened by God's truth in the gospel and to resolve to live truth."[6] As we discovered in Ephesians 1, we are redeemed by the blood of Christ. He paid the price of our ransom. It is only through faith in Jesus Christ that we come into relationship with God. Therefore, the first piece of armor is the truth. Jesus is the way, the truth, and the life! This is the belt that holds our spiritual armor in place.

> And you also were included in Christ when you heard the message of truth, the gospel of your salvation. When you believed, you were marked in him with a seal, the promised Holy Spirit.
>
> *EPHESIANS 1:13 NIV*

The Breastplate of Righteousness

Hand-to-hand combat was common for Roman soldiers; therefore, the breastplate, which covered the vital organs (heart, lungs, kidneys), was essential for survival. The same holds true for our spiritual armor. The primary place our enemy strikes is our heart, but God provides for us an abiding protection: the breastplate of righteousness.

Righteousness means to have a right standing before God. Think back to the story of the prodigal son who squandered his father's inheritance, which we read in Week 4. The son was covered in pig slop when he repented and returned home. When the prodigal was welcomed back into his father's home, he was covered with a new robe, which represented being "right" with his father and welcomed into the family. This guy did nothing to deserve this acceptance; he was welcomed home completely by grace. This illustrates God's grace in our lives and how Jesus makes us right with God. Our sin is covered with the righteousness of Christ.

Review Ephesians 1:4-7. What has Christ done for us?

> Therefore, having been justified by faith, we have peace with God through our Lord Jesus Christ.
>
> ROMANS 5:1 NASB

Do you see yourself as holy, blameless, and beloved by God? How could believing this truth transform your ability to resist the enemy?

At salvation, a "breastplate of righteousness" is issued to each person who trusts in Jesus as Savior. We are only righteous (or right with God) because we are "in Christ." Therefore, this piece of armor protects our hearts from the enemy's schemes of condemnation, shame, and accusation because it declares us not guilty before God.

Feet Fitted with the Gospel of Peace

If you've ever played the childhood game of tug-of-war, then you may recall how easy it is to lose your balance if your feet are not firmly planted. Ultimately, the team that fails to stand firm is the one who loses. The same was true in ancient warfare. When pitted against an enemy in combat, the soldier who stood firm until the end was the victor. For this reason, Roman soldiers wore sandals that wrapped tightly around the ankle and calf. The soles were fitted with sharp spikes that drove into the ground when the soldiers stood, enabling them to maintain firm footing when under attack. The ability to plant your feet and not fall is why this piece of our armor proves so vital.

Nothing can separate us from God's love!

The enemy loves to attack a child of God's sense of peace and security. Fiery arrows of fear and doubt rain down upon us. The enemy uses condemnation to cause doubt about our status as God's child and, consequently, about our well-being in this life. What, then, gives us sure footing when the enemy attacks? It is the knowledge that we are at peace with God because of our faith in Jesus (Romans 5:1).

How has the enemy used fear or anxiety in the past to torment you? (Be specific.)

When a woman's soul is at peace, she knows her status before God is secure. She knows she is His masterpiece in whom He delights.

She recognizes that this world is filled with trouble and heartache, but her God has overcome the world. This confidence brings security to every aspect of her being; and in the midst of life's trials, she knows that she belongs to Jesus. It is the peace of Christ that floods her heart when she remembers that nothing in this world can separate her from God's love.

Read Romans 8:31-39. This incredible passage speaks to God's unwavering love for us. How does this passage reinforce the fact that you have peace with God because of the gospel?

Friend, I've personally experienced the power that comes from putting on the armor of God, and I pray you do too. Declaring the truth of my identity in Christ broke the power of the enemy over my mind. The storm clouds lifted, and I experienced freedom from the accusations for the first time in weeks. Where my heart had known only fear of rejection and condemnation, I experienced the deep love of God and assurance that I was His masterpiece. As I planted my feet in the gospel, tightened the belt of truth, and guarded my heart with Jesus' righteousness, I experienced His victory. The enemy's power to harass me ceased when I chose to stand in my position as God's beloved child.

The same can be true for you. I pray you are encouraged today of your righteous standing before God. This truth covers our hearts from the fiery darts that are laced with fear and it fills us with peace as we plant our feet firmly in the fact that we belong to Jesus and nothing can separate us from His love!

Prayer

In the space below, connect with God using your own words:

DAY 3: THE ARMOR OF GOD, PART 2

Focal Point

Begin today's study by reading Ephesians 6:16-17.

Church culture was a prominent part of my childhood. Although I didn't personally trust Christ as my savior until I was an adult, I'm thankful for the foundation this upbringing provided. One activity I participated in as a child was an event called "sword drills." In case you aren't familiar, in a sword drill, the kids line up, the leader calls out a verse in the Bible, and the person who can flip through the flimsy pages fastest and find the verse wins.

The sad irony is this: although I could win at a game called sword drill as a child, when I became an adult I had no idea how to use the real sword of the Spirit. My life was crippled with insecurity, shame, and sin—a far cry from the victory that is ours in Jesus Christ. It wasn't until I began to follow Jesus and study His Word that I came to understand what this term "sword of the Spirit," found in today's Focal Point, actually means.

Yesterday we reviewed the pieces of armor that we wear at all times, and today we are delving into the three parts of the armor that we take up during battle. God has equipped us with armor to resist the enemy. Let's learn how to do just that!

Take Up the Whole Armor of God

To "take up" the whole armor means we aren't passive bystanders. One commentator notes, "'Take up' is a technical military term describing preparation for battle. The armor is available, but the believer-soldier must 'take it up' in order to be ready."[7] Since spiritual warfare is a reality we all encounter, let's turn our attention to the weapons we are to take up in time of need.

> Therefore take up the whole armor of God, that you may be able to withstand in the evil day, and having done all, to stand firm.
>
> *EPHESIANS 6:13 ESV*

Refer again to Ephesians 6:16-17. What three pieces of armor are "taken up" in the midst of battle? (vv. 16-17)

What is the purpose of the "shield of faith"? (v. 16)

What is specifically defined as the "sword of the Spirit"? (v. 17)

The Shield of Faith

Scripture cautions that we will be under attack from "flaming arrows of the evil one" (Ephesians 6:16 NIV). In ancient warfare, armies launched fire-tipped arrows at their opponents. Just imagine a soldier on a battlefield as those fiery darts rained down from above. The first instinct would be to seek cover and hide from the onslaught.

Although we don't face physical fiery darts, we do experience them in the spiritual realm. These fiery darts could be an onslaught of temptation or an intense struggle with an addiction. They also could be sudden attacks of doubt or an extreme struggle with jealousy, pride, insecurity, or anger. Fiery darts often take the form of mental assaults that hurl themselves against our minds. The bottom line is that the flaming arrows target our flesh (the old sinful nature) and seek to destroy our lives by luring us away from God.

A dear friend recently experienced a heartbreaking divorce. She is fighting to hold fast to God in the midst of a real battle for her heart. She shared how fiery darts of doubt, fear, and temptation strike her on a daily basis. Doubt about God's goodness. Fears concerning the future. And temptations to walk away from Jesus during this trial. She recognizes Satan's schemes. She shared how she is resisting the lure to soothe her heartache through alcohol and sexual sin. I'm so proud of how she is actively choosing to stand firm in moments of weakness.

What situation feels like fiery darts are aimed at your heart?

The shield of faith is perfectly designed to defend us against such assaults. But what is faith, and how does it cover us? Let's explore a few Scriptures to see how faith covers us in the midst of the fire.

The Big Picture

The Roman soldier's shield was not a small piece of metal in front of his body. His shield was more like a door held above his head to protect him from the flaming arrows falling from above.

The Big Picture

The Roman soldier's helmet "was made of bronze and was equipped with pieces of armor that were specifically designed to protect the cheeks and jaws. . . . This piece of armor was so strong, so massive, and so heavy that nothing could pierce it— not even a hammer or a battle-ax."[8]

What does Hebrews 11:1, 6 teach us about faith?

Put simply, faith believes God. Faith sees into the unseen realm and calculates God's goodness, power, and provision into every scenario. Faith holds fast to who God is. Although we can't see Him, we trust His character. When we lift up our shield of faith, we proclaim the greatness of our God to our own hearts and to the spiritual forces that oppose us.

Think of a battle you're currently facing. What specific truth about God can you lift high (like a shield) that will extinguish the flaming arrows of the evil one?

The Helmet of Salvation

To grasp the significance of the helmet of salvation, we must realize that our enemy specializes in discouragement. Our minds are bombarded with thoughts of despair, gloom, and dread. But, as believers in Jesus, joy is the hallmark of our faith and is rooted in the abiding hope we have in Christ. Therefore, the helmet of salvation is the key to our victory in the midst of darkness as it covers our minds and keeps us from surrendering to pessimism and the hopelessness that plagues our culture.

The helmet of salvation protects us from the schemes of discouragement because of the promise of our salvation. In Ephesians 6:17, the use of the word *salvation* proves a little confusing at first. Scripture speaks of salvation in three tenses: *past*, *present*, and *future*. Past-tense salvation is freedom from the penalty of sin. Present-tense salvation is the work of sanctification whereby we are being freed from the power of sin. Future-tense salvation is the glorious hope of all Christians that one day we will be free from the presence of sin; it is the hope of the new world God is preparing for us. So here in Ephesians 6:17, salvation is the future-tense, the one that looks forward in hopeful anticipation to the victorious return of Christ, which is to cover our thoughts and minds. It is only with a mind fixed on Jesus and His victory that we can overcome the darkness in this world by knowing that the future is indeed glorious because Jesus has won!

Read Isaiah 26:3 in the margin. What connection is made between our peace and our minds?

> You keep him in perfect peace whose mind is stayed on you, because he trusts in you.
> ISAIAH 26:3

Friend, the battlefield for our lives begins in our minds. I've experienced spiritual warfare on numerous occasions and can attest to the supernatural covering we have in the helmet of salvation. Fixing our minds on Jesus and the hope we have in Him protects our thoughts from the schemes of the enemy.

The Sword of the Spirit

Ephesians 6:17 teaches us that the sword of the Spirit is the Word of God, and Jesus modeled for us how to resist the enemy with it. Shortly after Jesus' baptism, He was led by the Holy Spirit into the wilderness where He was tempted by the devil. Before we dig into the details of this conflict, let's look at the context.

Read Matthew 3:13-17. What does the voice from heaven declare about Jesus' identity? (v. 17)

Jesus was identified as the beloved Son of God. This proves vital to understanding the goal of spiritual warfare: Satan tempts us to live contrary to who God says we are. This is why the apostle Paul diligently worked to teach our identity in Christ throughout this epistle. In the first two chapters of Ephesians we learn who we are "in Christ"—we are God's masterpiece. Finally, in chapter 6, we are told to stand firm against the forces that seek to hinder us from living this truth. Now let's see how Jesus resisted the enemy with the sword of the Spirit.

Read Matthew 4:1-11. How did Jesus respond to each of Satan's temptations? (vv. 4, 7, and 10)

It is only with a mind fixed on Jesus and His victory that we can overcome the darkness in this world by knowing that the future is indeed glorious because Jesus has won!

Concerning this showdown, one theologian writes, "Satan used three temptations: the temptation to turn stones into bread, the temptation to test God by jumping from the temple, and the temptation to escape the cross by falling down and worshiping Satan. Each of these temptations is related to what Jesus had heard from heaven at his baptism, namely, that he was God's 'Son' with whom God the Father was 'well pleased.'"[9]

Doubt was the enemy's game plan. Each time Satan spoke to Christ, he used the word *if*.

* If you are the Son of God, then . . . (Satan wanted Jesus to doubt his identity as the son of God.)
* If you will worship me . . . (Satan wanted Jesus to doubt his Father's plan and take a shortcut around the cross.)

In the garden of Eden account, in which the serpent is considered by many to be a representation of Satan, we see doubt used as a weapon of temptation against Adam and Eve. Satan's playbook hasn't changed. Doesn't that old "snake" do the same thing with you and me?

* If God really loved you, then . . .
    (A temptation to doubt God's heart for you.)
* If God is really good, then He wouldn't allow . . .
    (A temptation to doubt the character of God.)
* If you were really a Christian, then . . .
    (A temptation to doubt your own salvation.)

When has the enemy used doubt in your life?

Each time Satan tempted Jesus, Jesus replied to his suggestive questions with three simple words: "It is written," followed by a truth from Scripture that addressed the devil's lie. Finally, Jesus took authority over Satan and commanded him to leave. Guess what: in Christ we have that same authority. After all, Scripture tells us that he is under our feet (Romans 16:20)!

Friend, if we are to stand against the enemy as Jesus modeled for us, then it is imperative that we know the Word of God so that we can actively refute lies when they assail our hearts. While we can't stop spiritual warfare from occurring, we can stand victoriously when we know the truth and proclaim it in the midst of battle.

More Than Conquerors

The Bible doesn't sugarcoat the fact that spiritual warfare exits, but we are told in Scripture that we are more than conquerors in Christ and nothing can separate us from God's love (Romans 8:31-39)! We are equipped with the full armor of God to stand firm when the battle rages. You are a child of God Most High! Rejoice in the fact that your enemy is a defeated foe. The only power he has is to lie to us. And when we know God's truth, we hold the perfect weapon to resist him.

Prayer

In the space below, connect with God using your own words:

DAY 4: PRAYER, THE SUPERNATURAL FORCE

Focal Point

Begin today's study by reading Ephesians 6:18-20.

As I've mentioned previously, my first real prayer occurred in a bar, when I finally came to the end of myself and cried out to God for deliverance. That prayer was two simple words, "God, help." Now that I think about it, most of my prayers since that day can be summarized with the same simple phrase. While countless books have been written on this subject, the simple truth is this: in prayer, the power of heaven comes to earth. The impossible becomes possible. Prayer is engagement with the living God in which we bring our human weakness before the One who is all-powerful, all-knowing, and all-loving. At its core, prayer is not a list or a formality; it is weakness leaning on omnipotence. It is a child running to her father and crying out, "Daddy, help."

Throughout our study of Ephesians, we've taken a front-row seat to observe how the apostle Paul prayed and learned from his relationship with God. How fitting, then, that Paul closes Ephesians with an appeal to pray. After challenging us to take up the full armor of God to stand against the forces that oppose us, Paul then turns his attention to the supernatural power that we can access at any moment that connects us with the Lord God Almighty. As God's redeemed, prayer is our privilege, our power, and our priority in this world. Let's take a closer look at each of these truths.

Prayer Is Our Privilege as God's Child

Through our study, we have discovered a Father who moved heaven and earth to rescue those whom He calls His masterpiece. Paul, whose own eyes were opened to behold God's glory and see the supremacy of Christ, turned our eyes heavenward to marvel at God's love and brilliant plan to defeat our enemy. Through this, I pray that your image of God and understanding of His heart for you has changed or grown as you've seen His goodness revealed in the gospel.

Our view of God is paramount to how we engage with Him, especially in prayer. As A. W. Tozer rightly said, "What comes into our minds when we think about God is the most important thing about us."[10] If we do not see God as our loving Father and believe that we are His beloved children, then our prayers will be hindered by fear, shame, and unbelief. But if we hold fast to what we've learned in Ephesians, then our prayers will be bold and fueled by faith.

After spending six weeks studying Ephesians, how has your image of God changed?

In Week 2 of our study, we turned our attention the fact that God the Father chose us before the foundation of the world to be His own (Ephesians 1:3-6). This lavish love is the center of the gospel message and the primary truth of who we are in Christ—we are God's beloved masterpiece. Because we are loved, the Bible sets forth the reality that He desires us in His presence. As I've shared, the Lord has used the truths in Ephesians to heal my heart. One of the most profound and life-changing truths is that I am God's child and He delights in me. Simple, yes. But also, as Tozer said, the most important thing about me! This truth dismantled lies that declared I was unwanted and unloved. Now I know who I am and, as a result, I respond to God the Father as a beloved child instead of a nuisance or an unwanted annoyance. Truth changes everything! Our heavenly Father, who is the King of Glory, invites us to come boldly into His presence. He beckons us to come confidently to meet with Him. Friend, this access is our inheritance in Christ. Prayer is our privilege! We are both wanted and welcomed. Let that thought sink in for a minute.

Do you feel wanted and welcomed by God? Why or why not?

What typically hinders you from coming into His presence?

Read Hebrews 4:16. What instructions are given to us?

All that Paul has taught us in Ephesians about our new identity leads us to a new way to engage with God. We possess unhindered access to the throne of heaven. We don't need to go to another human to pray in our place, we don't need to clean ourselves up before we go to our Father, and we don't have to fear rejection— because we are God's beloved child. Once we believe this truth, truly own it as Ephesians has taught us to do, this knowledge brings boldness and expectancy in prayer.

Masterpiece Power

Motherhood is by far the most daunting job I've ever faced. In the weeks leading up to the birth of my daughter, I became increasingly aware of my shortcomings and lack of expertise. Anxiety clouded my mind during the final weeks of pregnancy. So, I took to social media asking for advice (rookie mistake) and came away with hundreds of posts offering conflicting sleep methods, feeding schedules, and ways of caring for a newborn. All of this contradictory information only added to my stress. *How would I know which method to use? Would I hurt my child if I picked the wrong one?* Throughout those weeks, I breathed out this simple prayer, "Lord, I need you!"

Once it was delivery time, I was still afraid but so ready to meet our girl! Praise God for the fantastic labor and delivery nurse He provided and for my kind husband who attended my every need—including playing worship music during the delivery.

I can't make this next part up. As I entered the final stage of labor, my doctor told me, "One more push, and you'll meet your daughter." Girls, I pushed with all my might. As I did, the playlist changed songs, and the song that just happened to play as my daughter was born was "Lord, I Need You." As I heard the familiar chorus, I looked at my husband to ask if he intentionally played the song, but he didn't. As my doctor lifted Sydney and placed her upon my chest, the words "Lord, I need you" echoed throughout the delivery room. I felt like God, my Father, winked at me and said, "I heard you."

Prayer is far more than just a formal event that occurs during our morning quiet time; prayer is the ongoing conversation we have with the Lord throughout the day as we face questions, needs, and challenges. He is with us. The Lord is our Helper, Shepherd, Guide, and Teacher. He knows all things and is our supply of strength, wisdom, and grace. The Lord knows the best sleep method for a particular baby. The Lord knows the best school for a child. The Lord is present and ready to help us in our weakness. When we talk to Him as we go, we engage with the Living God.

I've discovered the power of breath prayers—short prayers that fit into one inhale and exhale. God's wisdom and power are merely a breath away. Throughout Ephesians, we've learned we are God's masterpiece and our calling in this world is to showcase His glory. We can only do this by and in the power of His Spirit. When we stay connected to God throughout the day, we invite His Spirit to lead, guide, and teach us as we go. We welcome the Spirit to fill us and flow through us. This is how He empowers us to live for His glory.

Read Philippians 4:6-7. When are we to pray, and what result is promised to us when we pray?

Here are a few examples of breath prayers that help me stay in tune with God throughout the day:

> **"Speak, Lord, for your servant is listening."** Based on 1 Samuel 3:9, we can pray these words to quiet our souls and express our desire to hear from God.

> **"My help comes from the Lord, the Maker of heaven and earth."** I often pray this prayer of dependence, from Psalm 121:2 (NIV), when feeling overwhelmed. It reminds me that my help does not come from my own strength but from God Almighty.

> **"Not my will, but yours be done."** When life is challenging, I've learned to pray this simple prayer as a means of surrender to the Lord. This is a confession that God's ways are higher and better than my own.

> **"Jesus, Jesus, Jesus."** One of the most effective breath prayers is simply to speak out loud a name of God. When I sense I'm in the midst of a spiritual battle, or I'm in need of God's comfort, I simply (with reverence) call upon His name. When I do, I sense His presence and nearness. Proverbs 18:10 says, "The name of the LORD is a strong tower; the righteous man runs into it and is safe."

Our power to overcome the enemy and walk in victory, living as God's glorious masterpiece, is found in our abiding relationship with

Prayer is far more than just a formal event that occurs during our morning quiet time; prayer is the ongoing conversation we have with the Lord throughout the day.

Prayer is one of the most effective ways we can showcase God's goodness and grace to those who do not know Him.

Jesus. We are invited into a real relationship where we can walk with God and experience His power and presence. Prayer is the means in which we do so.

Review Ephesians 6:18-20. For whom are we to pray?

Here Paul calls upon us to pray and intercede on behalf of others. I firmly believe prayer is one of the chief ministries of a child of God. The command to pray is not for special groups of Christians but for all of us. We engage with God to bring His will upon the earth as we intercede for ourselves and others. There is no situation when prayer is not needed; after all, the great apostle said that we should pray "on all occasions with all kinds of prayers and requests" (Ephesians 6:18 NIV). Just imagine, God uses our prayers to change the trajectory of the world.

As a reminder of our priority in this world, read Ephesians 2:10. What are we created to do?

Good works are how we manifest God's glory to a lost world. Prayer is one of the most effective ways we can showcase God's goodness and grace to those who do not know Him.

A dear friend of mine uses prayer to minister to people. I've watched her listen to God and share with strangers what He speaks to her heart for them. For example, if we are in a restaurant, she will pray for the server and ask the Lord to give her a word for that person. Time and again, I've seen how this simple act speaks volumes to the recipient. Often that person feels unknown by God and experiences His tangible care for them through my friend who shares God's love for them. One time she walked up to a woman at a fast-food restaurant and said, "God loves you and sent me to pray for you." The woman burst into tears and shared how she was planning to commit suicide after her shift. Each time I see my friend minister to others this way, I think of Ephesians 2:10 and realize she is doing the good works that God created her to do.

Today we've looked at prayer—our privilege, our power, and our priority in this world. Let us always remember never to limit God when we pray. We speak to the One enthroned in heaven, the One who is the Creator of all things, and the One whom we call Daddy. Just as a good father loves to provide for and bless his children, so our good, heavenly Father stands ready to hear us and answer when we call.

Prayer

In the space below, connect with God using your own words:

DAY 5: LOVE INCORRUPTIBLE

Focal Point

Begin today's study by reading Ephesians 6:19-24.

As we turn the page to our final day of study in Ephesians, my heart brims with fresh passion for the glory of God. I'm more in awe of redemption today than I was when we began this journey and hope you are too. It is my sincere prayer that the Lord has ministered to you, encouraged you, and taught you the truth of who you are in Christ as His masterpiece. What an honor it has been to pour over God's Word with you these past six weeks. Now, as we draw our time together to a close, let's lean in and hear the apostle Paul's final words to his friends in Ephesus:

> *Grace be with all who love our Lord Jesus Christ with love incorruptible.*
> EPHESIANS 6:24 ESV

> ²⁰Now to him who is able to do immeasurably more than all we ask or imagine, according to his power that is at work within us, ²¹to him be glory in the church and in Christ Jesus throughout all generations, for ever and ever! Amen.
>
> *EPHESIANS 3:20-21 NIV*

As Paul bids farewell to his friends in Ephesus, he prays for God's grace to be with them and describes their love for the Lord Jesus Christ with a Greek word meaning "incorruptibility." Something that is "incorruptible" is "not subject to decay or dissolution."[11] Unlike most of the food in our refrigerators, this love does not spoil. I find that my fresh fruit rots before I have time to return to the store. How fitting that the great apostle Paul, who first established the church in Ephesus, praised his dear friends for their thriving and unspoiled devotion to Christ. I read those words as a challenge for my own relationship with Jesus. How can I love Jesus in such a way that my passion for Him never fades, corrupts, or grows stale? Ephesians holds the key.

As we continually turn our thoughts back to the beauty of the cross, the triumph of God's grace, and the glory of Jesus, then we grow to love Him more deeply and walk with Him more intimately. Truly, this epistle fans to flame a passion for God's glory like none other. Although our study of Ephesians is now complete, I pray you will treasure this letter all your days—returning to it time and again to behold the magnificence of the gospel and your calling as God's masterpiece.

We have a simple goal for our final day together—*to read all of Ephesians in one sitting.* I know you may be tempted to skip this assignment, but please don't! Now that we've studied it verse by verse and word by word, it is incredible how much more you will glean as you read it again as a whole.

Here are a few suggestions for gleaning the most from this exercise:

* Begin with prayer. Ask the Holy Spirit to illuminate Ephesians to you.
* Slow down and savor each word as you would a delicious meal.
* Stop when the Holy Spirit highlights something to you and write down what He reveals in the space below.
* As you finish reading the epistle, ask the Lord what insights or takeaways He wants you to apply in your life today.

Now, read Ephesians 1–6 and record your insights below and on the following page.

You are God's masterpiece! You were rescued by Christ Jesus to showcase God's glory to the world.

Friend, the truths in this epistle have been used by the Holy Spirit to transform my life from the inside out, and I pray He is doing the same for you. You are God's masterpiece! You were rescued by Christ Jesus to showcase God's glory to the world. I pray you will always remember and hold fast to your intrinsic worth, your identity as God's beloved child, and your calling to live as light in the midst of darkness.

For His Glory,

Marian

VIDEO VIEWER GUIDE ANSWERS

Session 1
Joy
royal announcement
status

Session 2
Hope
in Christ
glory

Session 3
saint
spiritually born
masterpiece

Session 4
position
surrender
loves Jesus
Holy Spirit

Session 5
look / gaze
love
forgiveness

Session 6
strong
armor
Stand firm

NOTES

WEEK 1

1 Robert M. Edsel, *The Monuments Men: Allied Heroes, Nazi Thieves, and the Greatest Treasure Hunt in History* (Little, Brown and Company; Media Tie In, Reprint edition, October 22, 2013).

2 *Holman Illustrated Bible Dictionary*, rev. and exp., "sin," ed. Chad Brand, Eric Mitchell, and Holman Reference Editorial staff (Nashville, TN: Holman Bible Publishers, 2015), 1477.

3 Author's definition.

4 James M. Boice, *Ephesians: An Expositional Commentary* (Grand Rapids, MI: Ministry Resources Library, 1988), 3.

5 Eugene E. Carpenter and Philip W. Comfort, *Holman Treasury of Key Bible Words: 200 Greek and 200 Hebrew Words Defined and Explained* (Nashville, TN: Broadman & Holman Publishers, 2000), 228.

6 Helen Starkweather, "Exploring Ancient Ephesus," *Smithsonian Magazine*, January 2008, https://www.smithsonianmag.com/travel/exploring-ancient-ephesus-11753958/, accessed December 12, 2019.

7 James M. Boice, *Acts: An Expositional Commentary* (Grand Rapids, MI: Baker Books, 1997), 328.

8 Boice, *Acts*, 323.

9 Boice, *Acts*, 329.

10 Bruce B. Barton and Philip W. Comfort, *Life Application Bible Commentary: Ephesians* (Wheaton, IL: Tyndale House Publishers, 1996), xvii.

WEEK 2

1 Neil T. Anderson, *Who I Am in Christ: A Devotional* (Bloomington, MN: Bethany House Publishers, 2003), 11.

2 Boice, *Ephesians*, 21.

3 M. G. Easton, in *Easton's Bible Dictionary* (1893; New York: Scriptura Press, 2015), 595.

4 Richard Booker, *Celebrating Jesus in the Biblical Feasts, Expanded Edition: Discovering Their Significance to You as a Christian* (Shippensburg, PA: Destiny Image Publishers, 2016), 40.

5 Warren W. Wiersbe, *The Bible Exposition Commentary*, vol. 2 (Wheaton, IL: Victor Books, 1996), 10.

6 John D. Barry, D. Mangum, D. R. Brown, M. S. Heiser, M. Custis, E. Ritzema, and others, *Faithlife Illustrated Study Bible* (Ephesians 1:14) (Grand Rapids, MI: Zondervan, 2017), 1940.

7 Wayne Detzler, *Living Words in Ephesians* (Hertfordshire, England: Evangelical Press, 1981), 25–26.

8 Billy Graham, *The Reason for My Hope: Salvation* (Nashville, TN: Thomas Nelson, 2013), 82.

9 Watchman Nee, *The Normal Christian Life* (Carol Stream, IL: Tyndale House Publishers, 1977), 41.

10 Klyne Snodgrass, *The NIV Application Commentary: Ephesians* (Grand Rapids, MI: Zondervan, 1996), 91.

WEEK 3

1 Wiersbe, *The Bible Exposition Commentary*, 18.

2 New Bible Dictionary, 3rd ed., s.v. "Sin," ed. Donald J. Wiseman, I. Howard Marshall, A. R. Millard, and J. I. Packer (Leicester, England; Downers Grove, IL: InterVarsity Press, 1996), 1105.

3 Watchman Nee, *Sit, Walk, Stand* (Carol Stream, IL: Tyndale House Publishers, 1977), 2.

4 Nee, *Sit, Walk, Stand*, 4.

5 "The Mona Lisa, by Leonardo Da Vinci," https://www.leonardodavinci.net/the-mona-lisa.jsp, accessed November 18, 2019.

6 "Leonardo's Masterful Technique," https://www.pbs.org/treasuresoftheworld/mona_lisa/mlevel_1/m3technique.html, accessed November 18, 2019.

7 Jerry Bridges, *Transforming Grace* (Colorado Springs, CO: NavPress, 1991), 144.

8 Rick Renner, *If You Were God Would You Choose You?: How to Accept, Pursue, and Fulfill the Call of God on Your Life* (Tulsa, OK: Teach All Nations, 2006), 245.

9 *The Lexham Bible Dictionary*, s.v. "Circumcision," *The Lexham Bible Dictionary*, ed. in J. D. Barry, D. Bomar, D. R. Brown, R. Klippenstein, D. Mangum, and C. Sinclair Wolcott, and others (Bellingham, WA: Lexham Press, 2016), 158.

10 "God's Covenant with Abraham," https://www.gospelproject.com/gods-covenant-with-abraham/, accessed November 18, 2019.

11 New Bible Dictionary, 3rd ed., ed. Donald J. Wiseman et al. (Leicester, England; Downers Grove, IL: InterVarsity Press, 1996), 199.

12 Bruce B. Barton, Philip W. Comfort et al., *Life Application Bible Commentary: Ephesians* (Carol Stream, IL: Tyndale House Publishers, 2001), 814.

13 Harold W. Hoehner, "Ephesians," in *The Bible Knowledge Commentary: An Exposition of the Scriptures*, vol. 2, ed. J. F. Walvoord and R. B. Zuck (Wheaton, IL: Victor Books: 1985), 630.

14 Wiersbe, *The Bible Exposition Commentary*, 31.

15 Barton and Comfort, *Life Application Bible Commentary: Ephesians*, 70.

WEEK 4

1 Boice, *Ephesians: An Expositional Commentary*, 121.

2 Rick Warren, "Day 19: Cultivating Community," *The Purpose Driven Life* (Grand Rapids, MI: Zondervan, 2002), 148.

3 "Gentleness," https://www.biblestudytools.com/dictionary/gentleness, accessed November 20, 2019.

4 "Rupertus Meldenius," https://www.ligonier.org/learn/articles/essentials-unity-non-essentials-liberty-all-things/, accessed November 20, 2019.

5 Nee, *Sit, Walk, Stand*, 3.

6 Barton and Comfort, *Life Application Bible Commentary: Ephesians*, 95.

7 Wiersbe, *The Bible Exposition Commentary*, 41.

8 Warren W. Wiersbe, *Wiersbe's Expository Outlines on the New Testament* (Colorado Springs, CO: Victor Books, 1992), 550.

WEEK 5

1 "The Question of God," https://www.pbs.org/wgbh/questionofgod/ownwords/mere2.html, accessed November 22, 2019.

2 Boice, *Ephesians*, 177.

3 "Cast Away FedEx Super Bowl Ad," accessed November 23, 2019.

4 Merriam-Webster Dictionary, s.v. "intoxicated," https://www.merriam-webster.com/dictionary/intoxicated, accessed November 23, 2019.

5 Snodgrass, *The NIV Application Commentary: Ephesians*, 289.

6 Andrew Murray, *Absolute Surrender* (Fort Washington, PA: CLC Publications, 2012), 5.

7 "Marriage Is a Mirror," https://www.thegospelcoalition.org/article/marriage-is-a-mirror/, accessed November 23, 2019.

8 "What Are Complementarianism and Egalitarianism?" https://www.christianity.com/wiki/christian-terms/what-are-complementarianism-and-egalitarianism-what-s-the-difference.html, accessed November 23, 2019.

9 "Wives: What Submission Does (and Doesn't) Mean," https://jdgreear.com/blog/wifely-submission-heres-really-means/, accessed November 23, 2019.

10 Barton and Comfort, *Life Application Bible Commentary: Ephesians*, 114.

11 Barton and Comfort, *Life Application Bible Commentary: Ephesians*, 120.

WEEK 6

1 "How to Survive a Lion Attack," https://www.smithsonianmag.com/smart-news/how-to-survive-a-lion-attack-6523224/#LMm9QPd4QGCh0hqh.99, accessed November 23, 2019.

2 "David Guzik: Study Guide for Ephesians 6," https://www.blueletterbible.org/Comm/guzik_david/StudyGuide2017-Eph/Eph-6.cfm, accessed November 23, 2019.

3 Steven J. Cole, "Lesson 55: Standing Strong, Standing Firm (Ephesians 6:10-11)," Bible.org, 2008, https://bible.org/book/export/html/22076, accessed November 23, 2019.

4 Chip Ingram, *The Invisible War: What Every Believer Needs to Know about Satan, Demons, and Spiritual Warfare* (2006; Grand Rapids, MI: Baker Books, 2015), 28.

5 Timothy J. Keller, "The Whole Armor of God," sermon, Redeemer Presbyterian Church, New York City, 32:46, January 19, 1992, https://gospelinlife.com/downloads/the-whole-armor-of-god-5672/.

6 Snodgrass, *The NIV Application Commentary: Ephesians*, 342.

7 Barton and Comfort, *Life Application Bible Commentary: Ephesians*, 131.

8 Rick Renner, "The Helmet of Salvation," Sparkling Gems from the Greek, August 4, 2016, https://renner.org/the-helmet-of-salvation/, accessed November 23, 2019.

9 James M. Boice, *The Gospel of Matthew: The King and His Kingdom, Matthew 1–17* (Grand Rapids, MI: Baker Books, 2001), 55.

10 A. W. Tozer, *The Knowledge of the Holy* (New York: Harper One Publishers, 1961; 2009), 1.

11 Merriam-Webster Dictionary, s.v. "incorruptible," https://www.merriam-webster.com/dictionary/incorruptible, accessed November 24, 2019.